Navigating the
Insurance
MAZE

The Therapist's complete Guide to Working With Insurance – And Whether You Should

By Barbara Griswold, LMFT

SECOND EDITION

Paper Street Press
San Jose, California
www.NavigatingtheInsuranceMaze.com

Navigating the Insurance Maze: The Therapist's Complete Guide to Working with Insurance – And Whether You Should.
By Barbara Griswold

© 2006, 2008 by Barbara Griswold
First Printing 2006
Second printing, revised 2008

Published by Paper Street Press
533 Patton Avenue
San Jose, CA 95128-2151
Printed in the United States of America
www.navigatingtheinsurancemaze.com

This manual is intended to provide information to assist psychotherapists in different situations related to working with private insurance plans. It is not intended to address every situation that could potentially arise, and is not a substitute for independent legal, financial, or clinical advice or consultation. This manual attempts to give a general overview of insurance plans; some plans will not fit the descriptions herein. Use of this manual does not substitute for reading individual provider or member contracts, or contacting the company for information on a specific plan or member's benefits. Be aware that laws, regulations, and technical standards vary with time and according to situational factors including the psychotherapist's license, state, and type and place of service. Thus, the reader should verify references or information contained herein.

ISBN: 978-0-615-19602-2

To my patient and selfless husband, Doug,
my daughter, Maria,
and my mom and dad,
who have supported me
in everything I've ever done.

How lucky am I?

Acknowledgments
ဆ ი

This book would not have been possible without Barbara Grover, LMFT.
Many of the concepts in the book were developed with Barbara
as we prepared for presentations on this topic.

For their thoughtful feedback and copy-editing of the first edition, I thank:
Karl Kahler, my editor,
Yvonne Blockie, LMFT,
Richard Ferry, LMFT,
and my mom, Marianne Corradi.

And for the generous contributions of their advice, time, and talents, I thank:
Susan Frager, LCSW, of Psych Administrative Partners, my billing guru, who saved me from
making huge (and potentially embarrassing) errors in my chapter on "double coverage,"
Mary Riemersma, Executive Director, California Assn. of Marriage & Family Therapists,
David Jensen and Michael Griffith, Staff Attorneys, California Assn. of Marriage & Family
Therapists,
Laynee Gilbert, LMFT,
all the therapists who contributed sample invoices and Superbills,
and all the folks at DeHart Printing, who patiently shepherded me through both editions of
this book.

Most of all I thank all of you whom I have had the pleasure to correspond with or meet at
my workshops. You remind me daily how much I have to learn, and keep me humble.

Table of Contents
ℬ ℭ

Introduction

৪১ ৫৩

"A successful therapy practice is one where you don't need to take insurance."

This comment sums up how many therapists feel about working with managed care plans. We often see accepting insurance in the same way struggling actors see waiting tables: It's a way to earn some extra income while making a name for ourselves.

I felt the same way in 1990, when I became licensed as a Marriage and Family Therapist and joined my first insurance provider networks. I wanted referrals, and figured I could always resign when my practice was full. Now, 18 years later, I am a provider for more than 20 insurance networks. While I long ago reached my goal of a self-sustaining practice, I only resigned from three networks along the way. Hopefully this book will explain why.

As I talk to colleagues and workshop attendees on the subject of insurance, it has become clear that while we make our living in the health field, many of us are in the dark about the most basic facts about health insurance and reimbursement. Why is this topic -- which has such a significant effect on the therapeutic relationship -- left out of the training of most interns, social work associates, and licensed therapists?

Despite (or perhaps because of) their lack of education on the topic, I find many therapists have made up their minds not to participate. A 2006 survey by the California Association of Marriage and Family Therapists showed that approximately 50 percent of their members are not affiliated with any managed health care provider networks[1]. Many clinicians have understandably been influenced by managed care horror stories. Fearing the compromise of confidentiality, loss of clinical control, increased paperwork, and discounted fees, many have chosen not to work with insurance. And those of us who do participate stumble along, learning from our mistakes, with little assistance in navigating the ethical, clinical, and administrative issues related to putting insurance into our practices.

This lack of a dialogue on the myths and realities of insurance is what led me to write this book. The goal of this manual is <u>not</u> to persuade you to accept insurance. It isn't right for everyone. On some days, I'm not even sure it was right for me. My aim instead is to give you some practical information you didn't get in graduate school. Once you understand what working with insurance entails, I hope you'll be able to decide whether it's a wise idea for your practice, based on facts instead of fears. After all, this is one of the most important business decisions you will make as a therapist. We all have clients who seek insurance reimbursement, so it is important that we understand how insurance works. In this case, what we <u>don't</u> know <u>can</u> hurt us – or our clients. And knowledge is power -- right?

I wrote this book in the first place because I am passionate about making the work we do accessible to those who can't pay $150 an hour, four times a month (hell, I couldn't even afford that!). I got into this profession to help others – not just those with lots of disposable income. While I know taking insurance is not the only way to help clients afford therapy, I find it hard to tell clients, who have paid big bucks for their insurance plans, that they can't use it to see me.

I write this second edition to update information from the first (things change so rapidly in the insurance field), to include more sample forms and letters to help guide you, to rid the text of embarrassing grammatical and spelling errors, and because in the last two years I've learned that some of what I wrote was just plain wrong.

Writing this manual has been a humbling experience for me: I learned how much I <u>didn't</u> know. This means that with any luck after you have read it you will know more than I did when I started to write it.

Barbara Griswold, LMFT

1
Why Take Insurance?
ೞ ೞ

As you traveled the long (it may have seemed unending) path toward licensure, perhaps you visualized your future psychotherapy practice. Maybe you dreamed of opening your own office. Of setting your own schedule. Of making a difference. Of having your own loyal and adoring clients. Most likely, you dreamed of a practice where each client paid out of pocket.

You probably didn't spend much time visualizing the business aspects of your future practice. It is likely your training concentrated on the clinical, the theoretical, the legal and ethical sides of the field, but you probably never took a course on how to start and maintain a small business. You may not even like to think of what you do as a business.

And that is why your visualization probably didn't include whether you'd take insurance. Perhaps you also heard stories from others that discouraged you from accepting insurance. The discounts. The paperwork. The limitations of coverage. The phone calls to check benefits and unsnarl claims problems. The need to discuss treatment decisions on occasion with case managers.

So, Why Consider Accepting Insurance?

Self-pay is no longer the norm. Therapists continue to want to focus on developing a self-pay-only practice, despite the fact that the number of clients who pay out-of-pocket is surprisingly small. A 2001 study of health spending showed that of all clients who sought treatment in the United States for mental health and substance abuse, only 12 percent paid out of pocket[2]. And a 2006 *Psychotherapy Finances* survey showed that the self-pay market is eroding. Most clinicians surveyed reported that they did not have as many self-pay clients as they did in 2000[3]. In fact, self-pay accounted for just 26 percent of the average therapist's private practice income, a decrease of 18% in just six years.

- **Insurance can be a great referral source.** When you become a preferred provider for an insurance company or employee assistance program, you may be contacted by clients who were given your name by their insurance plan. This can help fill those empty therapy slots. Since becoming very active with insurance, I get several calls each day from potential new insurance clients, and my practice is always full, with a waiting list. Now, this is not to say that this is everyone's experience, or that it will be yours. As they say, "your mileage may vary."

- **It may reduce your need for marketing and advertising.** Besides giving your name to clients who call asking for referrals, as a preferred provider the insurance plan may list your name on the insurance company Web site and in printed provider directories. If you hate advertising yourself, this is a nice benefit. "If you choose to let the insurance companies do the marketing, you will have more time to do therapy," says Casey Truffo, of BeAWealthyTherapist.com[4]. "Think of them as your sales staff. They work for you. You have basically hired them to do your marketing."

- **Insurance enables many clients to afford therapy.** With typical fees for self-pay clients averaging $95 to $125 per session, this places your talents out of the financial reach of much of the population. While they may love you and value therapy, it is a hard reality that some of my clients have to make the choice between seeing me and paying the rent. For them, paying my full fee – or even my sliding scale fee – cannot compare to paying their $10 co-payment. So if you want to make therapy affordable and accessible, and you want to see clients with a wide variety of issues and from diverse cultural and socioeconomic backgrounds, accepting insurance is one way to do that.

- **Or they can stay longer.** Even clients who can afford to pay privately for some amount of therapy may stay longer than they normally could afford to. I like to think of insurance as a type of subsidy, which aids clients in financing ongoing treatment.

- **It's a way to attract the "therapy-avoidant."** Having insurance coverage brings in clients who might never have come to therapy. This is especially true of employee assistance programs (EAPs), since they are usually a free benefit, advertised at the workplace. It may give clients a "taste of therapy," and they often choose to continue on their own after the EAP sessions have run out (for more about EAPs, see Chapter 3).

- **Holding on to clients, both old and new.** We've all had it happen – that great client who switches insurance companies, and tearfully informs you she has to leave since you don't take her new insurance, and she can't afford to pay out of pocket. Or the new client who calls after hearing great things about you, and ends up requesting a referral when he finds out you don't accept his insurance. Accepting a variety of insurance plans avoids these partings.

- **Free training.** Some insurance companies offer free or low-cost workshops or teleconferences for their participating providers on a wide variety of clinical issues. Some even offer free Continuing Education Units or pay you to attend. Many health plans put out regular provider newsletters, and post helpful online articles and resources for clients and providers.

- **Private practice can be isolating.** Believe it or not, sometimes it is helpful to have a case manager to discuss your client with, who might be able to help with treatment adjuncts, resources you didn't know about, or benefits you didn't know the client had.

- **My personal reason?** Gratitude. When I first saw a therapist, I was a full-time graduate student living on ramen and generic macaroni and cheese. My husband's insurance helped me afford the therapy that changed my life, in more ways than I can calculate.

2
Understanding Insurance Plans
Decoding the Alphabet Soup

ഇ ൦

There are few topics that stir such passionate feelings in the hearts of therapists as managed care and insurance. Much of our negative transference is related to the frustration of trying to learn how to deal with a system which can be very confusing, especially to the newcomer. Also, the rules vary among insurance companies, and with each type of plan, so it is nearly impossible to ever attain a feeling of competence.

To help you understand the types of insurance plans and the differences between them, it may help to use a case example.

Meet Jack

Jack comes to you at the urging of his wife, Jill. He reports he recently tripped over a pail of water and fell down a hill. Since the fall he has experienced recurring nightmares of the event, distressing recollections and flashbacks, hypervigilance, and has developed a phobic response when in the presence of a pail. Jack's anxiety has made it difficult to function in his job as a pail salesman at Pails "R" Us. Jack got your name from his insurance company, CureQuick Insurance.

First, A Few Definitions

As Jack investigates his insurance coverage, he is faced with learning a new vocabulary. While I've included an extended glossary at the back of this book to help you, let's start with some key concepts:

- **Deductible:** The dollar amount (usually yearly) that Jack has to pay before his insurance kicks in and begins to reimburse him for medical expenses. Not all plans have deductibles.

- **Co-payment:** The <u>fixed, flat fee</u> that Jack's plan may require him to pay for each visit (after the deductible is exhausted, if any). The insurance company pays the rest.

- **Co-insurance:** In some plans, instead of a fixed co-payment, Jack would pay some <u>percentage</u> of the provider's fee (after the deductible is exhausted, if any). Insurance pays the rest.

- **Provider network or panel:** These are the providers (LMFTs, LCSWs, psychologists, psychiatrists, etc.) who have signed a contract with CureQuick to deliver services to Jack and other members of the CureQuick health plan. The providers usually agree to accept a fee discount and to file claims for the clients in exchange for referrals from CureQuick.

Types of Mental Health Coverage

Jack is delighted to find out from a coworker that Pails "R" Us has an employee assistance program. This program entitles all employees and dependents to three free sessions yearly with a counselor in CureQuick Insurance's Employee Assistance Program network.

Employee Assistance Program (EAP): This is a benefit provided by employers who have prepaid to cover all employees and dependents for a certain number of free counseling sessions per year (usually three to ten) with one of their EAP network providers. EAP therapists provide assessment, short-term counseling, and referral.

An employee assistance program may be provided <u>instead of</u> other mental health coverage ("stand-alone coverage") or <u>in addition to</u> the employee's other mental health benefits. In the latter case, clients might be eligible to use their free EAP sessions before they begin using their other mental health benefits.

For more on EAPs, see Chapter 3, "Employee Assistance Programs."

After looking into it further, Jack is happy to learn that after the EAP sessions he also has ongoing mental health coverage through CureQuick Insurance. However, he learns that CureQuick has many types of health insurance plans, and Pails "R" Us offers more than one type of plan to employees. He can't recall which he signed up for during enrollment time.

After his EAP sessions are completed, Jack may have any one of the following common types of mental health coverage. A chart follows this section that compares the different features of each plan. Keep in mind that these are outlines only. Individual plans vary greatly and many types of insurance are not covered in this manual, including state and federal government plans.

Traditional Indemnity/Fee-for-Service Plan: Back in what some therapists recall as "the good old days" (that is, before the advent of managed care), insurance plans were mostly of this type. Now somewhat rare, these plans indemnify, or reimburse, the member or provider for health care expenses as they are incurred. There is no provider network -- Jack would be free to choose any providers he wants to see, see them as often as he likes, and after he satisfies his deductible and pays his co-payment, eligible services would be covered by his insurance plan. The provider's treatment is not reviewed by the plan. However, Jack may have to pay the provider's full fee at the time of service, and file claims for reimbursement to the insurance company. The plan typically would not cover preventive care services. Also, the plan may only cover what it considers to be "usual, customary and reasonable" fees (UCR), and he'll have to make up the difference. Bottom line: These plans offer flexibility in exchange for high out-of-pocket expenses, more paperwork, and higher premiums for the client.

Managed Care Plans: As health care costs rose each year, insurance companies responded by changing the structure of health plans. These new "managed" plans reduced costs in a variety of ways, including setting yearly session or spending limits, getting providers to accept discounts, and requiring pre-authorization (pre-treatment approval from the insurance company) and treatment review. It would be impossible to list all managed care plan varieties and details, so the most common types are outlined below.

1. **Health Maintenance Organization (HMO):** A HMO typically covers a higher degree of preventive care than other plans, in order to minimize later care costs. Jack must choose a primary care physician (PCP) who coordinates his care and makes referrals to specialists (though typically Jack would not need a referral to see a therapist). A HMO may have central medical clinics such as those used by Kaiser Permanente, or it may contract with a network of individual practices. HMOs usually offer broader coverage and lower out-of-pocket expenses for the client than other plans. However, many clients don't realize that with a HMO the insurance company will cover only visits to network providers, and their care may undergo more scrutiny than with other plans. For the provider, HMOs typically represent the highest amount of oversight and case paperwork. For the client, it is usually the least expensive but least flexible health plan.

2. **Preferred Provider Organization (PPO):** PPOs are generally less flexible than indemnity insurance but more flexible than HMOs. With a PPO, the insurance company will cover Jack's visits both to network and out-of-network providers, with higher benefits paid when he visits network providers. If he chooses a network provider, Jack will get the benefit of a participating provider fee discount, a lower co-payment and deductible, and the provider will file claims. However, this option usually involves deductibles (typically $100-$2500) and larger co-payments than HMOs. The provider's treatment is seldom reviewed by the company, and case paperwork is usually limited to claim forms.

3. **Exclusive Provider Organization (EPO):** An EPO operates like a PPO, except that the insurance company will only cover Jack's visits to network providers. As with PPOs, he will get the benefit of a participating provider discount, and the provider will file claims. Jack typically won't need a PCP referral but will usually be responsible for paying a co-payment and deductible.

4. **Point-of-Service Plan (POS):** A sort of HMO/PPO hybrid, this plan offers a great deal of flexibility and choice. With a typical POS plan, Jack would have a two- or three-tiered plan, and could choose any of the benefit levels when seeking care. He could choose a therapist from Tier 1, which would allow him to choose any therapist on CureQuick's HMO panel, and the plan would operate just like a normal HMO. He may instead obtain treatment from any participating provider in Tier 2, CureQuick's PPO network, and the plan would then work like a normal PPO. Finally, he may have a third tier, permitting him to go outside of both networks, and be reimbursed when he sees any licensed provider. If he chooses Tiers 1 or 2, Jack will get the benefit of a participating provider discount, and the provider will file claims. Each tier typically represents higher out-of-pocket expenses than the one before it.

Confused? Let's put the different plans side by side and compare them.

A Comparison of Typical Insurance Plans

	Are Out-of-Network Providers Covered?	Client's Usual Cost For Service	Who Files Claims?	Treatment Pre-Authorization Required?
EAP	No	Usually free, paid for by employer	Provider	Yes
Indemnity/ Fee-for-Service	There is no provider network—all providers are covered	Deductible, then a certain percentage of all expenses	Usually client	No
HMO	No	Typically lowest co-payments, usually no deductible	Provider	Sometimes, but depends on plan
PPO	Yes, but at a lower rate	Usually deductible, lower costs for network providers, higher costs for out-of-network providers	Provider, though client generally does if visiting an out-of-network provider	No
EPO	No	Typically have deductible and co-payment	Provider	No
POS	Yes, but at a lower rate	Lowest costs for HMO providers, higher for PPO providers, highest for out-of-network providers	Provider, though client generally does if visiting an out-of-network provider	May be needed if using HMO provider

Plans vary greatly. Please consult the specific health care policy or contract for plan details.

Getting Involved
Making Choices That Fit Your Practice

Hopefully you can see that as a therapist you have a lot of choice about how involved to get with insurance.

Your first decision will be whether to become a network provider, or to accept insurance as an out-of-network therapist, or some combination of these two options (though remember, not all plans cover out-of-network providers). Let's review.

If You are a Network (or Panel) Provider

- **Pros:** You will get new client referrals from the insurance company and their Web site; this may reduce your need for marketing. You'll be able to retain clients who have insurance and can't afford to pay privately.
- **Cons:** You must sign a contract with the plan. You typically accept a discounted rate for services, and must bill the insurance plan yourself. You may not "balance-bill" the client; that is, you cannot bill your client for the portion of your full fee that insurance doesn't pay since you agreed to accept the discount. Treatment may need to be pre-authorized and reviewed.

If You are an Out-Of-Network Provider:

- **Pros:** You don't need to sign a contract with the insurance plan. You do not have to discount your fee – you may collect from the client whatever portion of your full fee that the insurance doesn't pay. You have the option of collecting any deductibles and co-payments and billing the insurance plan for your clients, or having clients pay you in full and give them an invoices (also known as a "Superbill") to submit themselves (see sample invoice on Page 147). Your treatment usually will not need to be pre-authorized or reviewed.
- **Cons:** You won't get new client referrals from the insurance company – you'll need to market your practice. Clients may leave you (or not come to you) and instead find a network provider on their plan, since this may be substantially less expensive for them.

It's important to keep in mind that whenever you bill insurance your treatment is subject to review, whether or not you are a network provider.

The chart on the following page is another way of looking at your choices. It outlines the choices of two therapists who have selected different involvement levels with managed care, and how those decisions work for them.

Nina has decided she wants to take insurance but doesn't want to join any provider networks. She wants to avoid the paperwork and discounts she knows are part of the managed care world, so she chooses to be an out-of-network provider only.

Mark has gone for insurance "whole hog." He joins every network that will take him, hoping to fill those empty slots in his practice. He is willing to do the paperwork, and take some discounts in exchange for the referrals.

A Tale of Two Therapists: Two Extremes of Provider Participation

	Nina (No Managed Care): Out-of-Network Provider only	Mark (Managed Care): Network Provider
Accepts What Insurance Plans?	• Indemnity plans • PPO out-of-network • POS out-of-network	• EAP • HMO • PPO in-network • POS in-network • EPO • Indemnity plans
How Much Can Therapist Charge?	Full fee-for-service. Can bill client for whatever insurance doesn't pay	Except with indemnity plans, usually agrees to accept discounted fee. Cannot bill clients to make up for any fee discount
Amount of Paperwork	Typically minimal, may only involve claim form or invoice/superbill (see invoice sample on Page 147)	Minimal with indemnity plans. Otherwise, depends on company. Once accepted on panel, paperwork may include surveys for client to complete, claims, written requests for more sessions, and case summaries
Must Therapist Submit Claims?	No. You can collect co-payments and bill insurance, or accept full fee and give client an invoice or superbill to submit to the plan (see sample invoice Page 147)	Yes
Will Insurance Refer Clients?	No	Yes directly (phone) and indirectly (via printed or online provider directories)

A New Type of Health Plan: Tax-Advantaged Savings Accounts

As employers look for new ways to share the burden of rising health costs with their employees, some new types of plans have emerged. Some employers offer these instead of more traditional health plans.

1. <u>Health Savings Accounts (HSA) or Medical Savings Accounts (MSA)</u>: A health savings account allows an employee to set aside pre-tax dollars for future medical expenses. Contributions can be made by your client, his employer, or both. If Jack had an HSA, he would be given choices on how to invest these funds, and then could use them for qualified health expenses during the year. If he chose to save the money for future health expenses, the account would grow through investment earnings. The funds can roll over from year to year and are portable. He could take them with him if he changed jobs, changed medical coverage, became unemployed, or moved. He would need to be enrolled in a high-deductible health plan (in 2008 the minimum was $1,100 for an individual plan or $2,200 for a family) and he could have no other major insurance coverage. HSAs allow a lot of choice, including how much to put in the account, what expenses to pay out of it, and what investments to make. Jack could even  use the funds to pay for health expenses his insurance doesn't cover (such as for over-the-counter medications or bandages), or save the money for future health needs. And because of the high deductible, Jack may have a very low premium.

   Perhaps the most attractive benefit of all? The account provides Jack with triple tax savings: deductions when he contributes to the account, tax-free earnings through investment, and tax-free withdrawals for qualified medical expenses.

   United Behavioral Health Plan states that some of its plans allow clients to use the money in these accounts to reimburse providers directly for their portion of the costs[5]. Clients may have access to these accounts via checks or debit cards, so you could be reimbursed in this way. In addition, some plans will even require that you bill the health plan before a member is charged; check with the health plan in advance for instructions.

2. <u>Health Reimbursement Arrangements (HRA)</u>: The main difference between a HRA and an HSA is that HRA funds are provided only by an employer for an employee.

3. <u>Flexible Spending Accounts (FSA):</u> This account allows for reimbursement of dependent care and health care expenses, and enables employees to pay for these expenses with a non-taxed portion of their salary. The main difference between a FSA and a HSA is that FSA funds must be used within the calendar year or they are forfeited. Therefore, if Jack guesses he will be paying about $2000 in the coming year for child-care and medical expenses, he will have his employer deduct this amount from his salary over the course of that year. His employer would deposit these pre-tax payroll deductions into his (non-interest-bearing) FSA. Anytime Jack submits an invoice from a medical or child-care provider, he would be reimbursed with funds from his account. A client with an FSA does not need a high-deductible insurance plan.

3

Employee Assistance Programs
A Closer Look

✲ ☙

As mentioned in the previous chapter, an employee assistance program is a benefit provided by employers who have typically prepaid to cover all their employees and dependents for a certain number of free counseling sessions per year (usually three to ten) with one of their EAP network providers. EAP therapists provide assessment, short-term counseling and referral. By offering this program to their workers, employers hope it will improve productivity, minimize absences, and in other ways contain the employer's cost of illness.

An employee assistance program may be provided <u>instead of</u> other mental health coverage ("stand-alone coverage") or <u>in addition to</u> other mental health benefits. In the latter case, clients might be eligible to use their free EAP sessions before they access their other mental health benefits.

Jack's company, Pails "R" Us, may have an internal EAP, in which the EAP counseling office is located at the workplace, and where the EAP therapists are on the company payroll. Or the EAP may be external, made up of a network of community providers. In this case, Pails "R" Us hired CureQuick to provide both EAP benefits and ongoing mental health insurance and for its employees. Sometimes you will see the employer has hired a separate firm to provide EAP services.

It is unfortunate that not everyone has an employee assistance program. It is also unfortunate that clients who <u>do</u> have this benefit often aren't aware of it. So when you call the client's insurance company to ask about coverage, be sure to ask if he has this benefit. However, the EAP plan may be handled by a separate firm, so the company that handles a client's mental health benefits may not be aware of other coverage. You might then suggest that the client talk to his employer's human resources department or check his employee benefits manual.

Clients are often pleasantly surprised to find out that their EAP plan may offer other types of assistance, such as a few free sessions of legal consultation, financial advice, credit counseling, tax assistance, elder or child-care referral assistance, educational support and referrals, mediation services, and retirement planning. However, these visits may count against the client's total number of allotted EAP sessions.

When a client uses an EAP, it is important to keep in mind:

- Pre-authorization is always needed.

- There is no "out-of-network" EAP option. Clients must see a participating EAP provider.

- EAP sessions are typically free for the client.

- **Sessions are typically very limited in number.** You don't usually have the option of getting more until the following year. Sometimes if there is a new presenting issue they will allow you to count this as a separate event, and grant additional sessions.

- **Sessions are confidential.** EAP clients often worry that what they share will be shared with their employers. This is not the case, though different rules apply if counseling is mandated by the workplace or court (for more on confidentiality, see Chapter 15).

- **No diagnosis of mental illness is necessary.** Clients may see an EAP therapist to discuss any issue, and need not have a diagnosis. This is not the case with other types of mental health coverage. In addition, the sessions don't need to be "medically necessary" (more on this in Chapter 9).

- **Your role as an EAP provider is to provide assessment, referral, and brief problem resolution.** "It is especially important that EAP providers operate somewhat differently than they would during long-term treatment," says Managed Health Network. "EAP providers are most effective when they think of themselves as the early architects of a member's recovery rather than the means to that recovery[6]." Be sure to set realistic goals and treatment plans within the given time frame. If the client continues in therapy past the EAP sessions, goals can be modified at that time.

- **Follow-up may be expected.** As an EAP provider you may be expected to follow-up with clients after the EAP sessions are over if a referral was made (and sometimes even if no referral was made). Document any follow-up (or attempts) in the client's record. You may also be expected to call the health plan and close the EAP case when you are done. Some even expect a brief summary of treatment.

Questions and Answers

I'm confused. Sometimes "EAP" seems to be used to refer to the program. At other times it seems to refer to the counselor working in the program.

You're right – and it can be confusing. The initials EAP may stand for "employee assistance program," or it may refer to "employee assistance professional," the title of the clinician providing the services for the employee assistance program.

Can anyone apply to become an EAP provider?

It depends on the network. Some plans are simply looking for providers who can demonstrate experience and/or education in assessment, short-term problem resolution and referral. They want to see good brief therapy and crisis intervention skills, and chemical dependency assessment experience. Others require extensive EAP experience or training before they will put you on their "sub-network" of EAP providers. This makes getting your foot in the door more of a problem. Value Options health plan, for example, requires either 1) active status as a Certified Employee Assistance Professional (CEAP), or 2) two years of verifiable experience as an internal EAP counselor, and/or as an external EAP consultant to other organizations[7]. In addition, if you are not a CEAP, Value Options requires coursework, certification, or work experience in the assessment and treatment of substance abuse. Managed Health Network requires CEAP status or "1,500 hours of combined training and experience that resulted in expertise in the following areas: addiction counseling, job-related issues/performance improvement, short–term counseling, family and relationship counseling, assessment and referral[8]."

Can Jack get more EAP sessions after he has used his maximum, if he needs them?

Clients are usually limited to one batch of free sessions per year. However, some EAP benefits are not "per benefit year," they are "per incident," or "per problem type." Under these plans, Jack could use his EAP benefits more than once a year if he had different presenting issues on intake. Even with these types of plans, many EAP programs have a maximum number of allowable sessions per "contract year" (contracts are not always based on a calendar year). Some clients -- especially those in high-stress or high-risk jobs, such as police, firefighters, and paramedics -- may have EAP plans that allow them to access the EAP anytime they are adversely affected.

Why was my client referred directly to her ongoing mental health coverage for treatment, rather than to her EAP?

The insurance company's intake counselor may refer clients who have suicidal or homicidal ideation, severe or chronic mental illness, active substance abuse, or the need for immediate intensive treatment directly to their mental health coverage. They are not appropriate for the short-term focus of the EAP plan.

Can I just bill the EAP as I would for any other insurance session?

This depends on the plan. Many EAPs have their own claim forms, which they'll often send with the authorization. You will sometimes be asked to wait to bill for sessions until all EAP sessions are completed. You may need to attach a closed case form or case information form summarizing treatment. Many companies will not pay without these forms. If the client has both EAP and ongoing mental health benefits with the same company, and both allow you to use a universal CMS-1500 claim form (more about this in Chapter 11), it is wise to bill the EAP sessions on a separate page to avoid confusion. Also, some plans may require you to use a different CPT code for EAP sessions (more on CPT codes in Chapter 11). As usual, ask the plan.

What other roles do EAP providers play?

EAP therapists also assist employers by providing Critical Incident Stress Debriefings (CISD), consultations to employers, and mandated trainings (e.g. sexual harassment or chemical dependency), and employee mental health education seminars, and represent the EAP at employee health fairs.

Will EAPs pay for missed appointments or late-cancelled sessions?

Usually not, but check your contract. Some will deduct a session from the client's total EAP benefit for each missed session. Some programs will not allow you even to bill the client for the missed EAP session. Others allow you to bill the client if the client has previously agreed (in writing) to pay for missed sessions.

What are Jack's options if he needs further treatment when his EAP sessions end?

One of the following scenarios is possible for Jack:

1. Jack's CureQuick EAP sessions may be all the mental health coverage he has. You will have to refer him to appropriate and affordable community resources, or, if allowed, it may be possible to continue to see him in your self-pay practice (see next question below).
2. Jack may have further mental health benefits, also handled by CureQuick. You might then refer him to a CureQuick network therapist, possibly even yourself.
3. Jack may have further mental health benefits, handled by another insurance company. You might then refer him to a therapist within the other company's network, possibly even yourself.

So, Jack can continue working privately with me after the EAP sessions are over?

Well, that depends. Some companies have no problem with "self-referral". Treatment must, of course, be within the scope of your competence and practice, and it is wise to give alternate referrals. However, many companies do not allow self-referral: They do not want referral decisions to appear clouded by a therapist's desire to fill an empty therapy slot in his or her practice. The professional guidelines of the Employee Assistance Professionals Association state that "any actual or perceived conflict of interest among EAP professionals and service providers shall be avoided[9]." Value Options health plan states that some of the employers they work with do not allow it, some do. Once again, contact the insurance company to ask their policy.

Even companies that do not allow self-referral may make exceptions in certain situations. These situations may include when:

1. Continuity of treatment would enable successful and most rapid closure of clinical issues.
2. Disruption of service with you might place the client at risk.
3. You are working on an issue in which you possess an unusual expertise.
4. There are no available participating network providers in the same geographic area.

The self-pay agreement: If Jack has no further coverage, but wants to continue to see you (and your EAP contract allows self-referral), it is a good idea to have him sign a self-pay agreement (a sample agreement can be found on Page 145). This agreement states that he understands his therapy is no longer covered by insurance, and he is now responsible for paying your full fee (or one that you have negotiated with him).

If I see Jack as a self-pay client after the EAP, can I charge my usual fee?

Usually, yes. However, I know of at least one EAP firm whose contract states that if you continue privately with Jack after his EAP sessions, you must stick to the EAP discounted rate for these private sessions. For this type of contract, if you have discounted your rate to $62 for CureQuick's EAP clients, you may only charge Jack $62 if you continue to see him in your private practice when his EAP benefits have ended.

What about management referrals or supervisor referrals?

Managers, supervisors, and human resources personnel can formally refer employees whose personal problems are affecting work performance. These management referrals require special handling. They may involve voluntary attendance by the employee, but an employee may not be able to return to work and may be on unpaid leave until he reports to an EAP counselor or completes treatment.

Contrary to popular belief, in most cases the EAP counselor is <u>not</u> expected (or even allowed) to contact the supervisor or employer directly. Attendance and/or progress information is given only to the EAP case manager. What will the case manager tell the supervisor or manager? A typical policy is articulated by Value Options EAP in their client treatment agreement: "If you were formally referred to EAP by your supervisor, he or she will be provided the following non-clinical information: a) whether or not you have followed through in contacting the EAP; b) whether or not a problem has been identified and if a program treatment has been recommended; c) whether or not you are participating and complying with your treatment plan. Note: your supervisor will <u>not</u> be given clinical information about the specifics of your problems.[10]"

In our example Jack would sign a release of information to allow his employee assistance program administrators (not you) to speak with his supervisor or manager. The release is limited to the information outlined above. Even though the client may understand that in these cases the sharing of information is a condition of treatment, it is a good idea to discuss the types of information you are being asked to release, and to whom you will be releasing it, and have the client complete you own release of information before making any disclosures.

If a client expresses concern about harassment issues, worker's compensation, or company wrongdoing, or legal action, this may limit their confidentiality. It is advised that you talk to the client about these confidentiality issues, and talk to the case manager before making recommendations to the client that would support pursuing litigation or filing complaints against the employer or insurance company.

What if Jack asks me to write a letter excusing him from work? What if I am asked to fill out disability paperwork or fitness-for-duty determinations?

The EAP is not a medical service, so providers can't fill out disability paperwork or determine if an employee is fit for duty. You should avoid any verbal or written correspondence with the client's employer regarding the client's ability to work or any other aspect of treatment. This is usually outside the scope of our practice and training as psychotherapists, and is better left for the client's doctor or psychiatrist. You may be asked to answer questions for a state or private disability firm about the client's symptoms if the disability is related to mental health, but avoid subjective comments or making evaluations of fitness.

4

Horror Stories: Myth or Reality?

ඊ ගි

When therapists explain why they have chosen not to accept insurance, it often becomes clear that their decision was based on misinformation or myths. Let's explore some myths about getting involved with insurance:

<u>Myth</u>: "If I take insurance, I'll have to do billing, and lots of paperwork.

<u>Fact</u>: There's no denying that insurance involves paperwork. How much depends on your choices. If you loathe the idea of billing, you can choose to take insurance as an out-of-network provider. You can then collect your full fee from Jack and provide him with an invoice or superbill he can submit to CureQuick (see sample invoice Page 147) or you may choose to collect co-payments from Jack and submit the claim form for him. Either way, the paperwork is limited to one claim form or invoice.   Or, if you want referrals but minimal paperwork, you might join a few PPO networks.   Or you can simply limit the number of insurance clients you take, so that the paperwork is also limited.

<u>Myth</u>: "If I take insurance, I'll have to discount my fee."

<u>Fact</u>: As was discussed in Chapter 2, you only need to take fee discounts when you become a participating provider.   Let's say Jack has a PPO that covers 80 percent for network providers but only 50 percent for out-of-network providers. As an out-of-network provider, you could simply collect your full fee (e.g. $100) from Jack and provide him with a statement he can submit to CureQuick. Another option would be to collect from Jack his portion of your full fee (50%, or $50) and submit bills to CureQuick yourself for the balance ($50).

Should you choose to become a preferred provider, there is no getting around it — the reduced fee is by far the biggest complaint of most panel therapists. But some therapists feel it may be worth taking the discount for the referrals, and for the other reasons outlined in Chapter 1.

<u>Myth</u>: "If I take insurance, I'll have to do brief therapy, and sessions will be limited."

<u>Fact</u>: It's a fact: Insurance plans are looking for therapists who are skilled in short-term therapy. However, this doesn't mean they won't cover long-term treatment. Many plans allow unlimited sessions. Others may allow 50 sessions per year, which permits almost weekly sessions. Even if Jack is limited to 20 or 30 sessions per year, he may exhaust these benefits and then pay out of pocket until his benefits restart the following year, thus enabling you to provide long-term therapy. Even in plans where your treatment is reviewed by the managed care plan, often you

can continue to see clients as long as they are demonstrating "medical necessity" for treatment (more about this in Chapter 9).

Even clients with session limits often have what is called parity coverage. In most states (and in many insurance plans) mental health parity laws require that the plans provide coverage for certain mental health diagnoses on par with medical conditions covered by the plan. These laws attempt to change traditional coverage structures, where mental health benefits often had a lower reimbursement rate and more restrictions than medical benefits. Why does this matter to you? Certain clients with parity plans may be entitled to smaller co-payments and longer-term or even unlimited sessions. This may depend on the client's diagnosis. For an in-depth look at what every therapist should know about parity laws, see Chapter 7.

<u>Myth:</u> "If I take insurance, my therapy will be micro-managed by idiots at the insurance companies."

<u>Fact:</u> Contrary to common belief, case managers are often licensed Master's-level clinicians, not monkeys wielding a red "denial" stamp. Also, managed care companies tend to overwhelmingly approve most requests for additional sessions. Though they may call to discuss complex, lengthy, or chronic cases, such treatment reviews are probably rarer than most therapists imagine. In the 18 years I have worked with these plans, I have only been reviewed a handful times, and I have never felt micro-managed. I send in my treatment requests, they are typically approved, and I have little contact with case managers.

<u>Myth:</u> "All the networks are full."

<u>Fact:</u> While it is true that many insurance provider panels are full, there are always new openings. If you read any issue of *Psychotherapy Finances* (see Resources, Page 133), each month there is a list of panels that currently are looking for providers. Even those that are full today have changing needs. The plan may land a new employer account in your area tomorrow, and be scrambling to dig through resumes on file for providers with your ZIP code.

<u>Myth:</u> "If I take insurance, my clients will have to get a doctor referral to see me."

<u>Fact:</u> Eons ago, a pre-treatment doctor referral was required by many insurance plans, so this impression persists. However, managed care philosophy has changed, and almost all plans now allow client self-referral. In fact, none of the 20 plans I work with require doctor referral.

<u>Myth:</u> "If I take insurance, I'll have to give diagnoses to clients who aren't mentally ill."

<u>Fact:</u> While it is true that health plans generally only cover mental illnesses, this is not the case with employee assistance programs. It is insurance fraud to give a diagnosis where none exists. If you cannot justify a diagnosis, the client can always choose to pay out of pocket. Do not fall into the trap of giving each client the same diagnosis, one you feel can't hurt them. This is fraud.

<u>Myth:</u> "If I take insurance, I'll have to deal with HIPAA."

<u>Fact:</u> Taking insurance does *not* automatically mean you become a "covered entity" under the Health Insurance Portability and Accountability Act (HIPAA), or that you have to comply with the requirements of HIPAA. HIPAA only affects you if you will be communicating any confidential client information electronically (usually via the Internet) or if you have someone else conducting these transactions electronically on your behalf. However, there are some good reasons why all therapists should become knowledgeable about and compliant with HIPAA regulations. For more information about HIPAA, see Chapter 7.

5
Becoming a Network Provider
Selling Yourself to Insurance Companies

ℰℴ ℭℬ

It is said that in the "good old days," all you needed to join a provider network was a pulse. While that may be an exaggeration, many panels required little more than an application and resume. Those days are gone. In most areas of the country, if the network isn't already full, insurance companies can afford to be choosy, in part because there are more therapists applying.

Since it costs managed care companies to develop and maintain a provider network and database, it is in their best interest financially to maintain the fewest number of providers on their network. However, many managed care companies are required to maintain minimum "density standards" (the required number of providers in any given region), and must meet the varied clinical needs of their members in your area.

So, let's say you have decided to join a provider panel. Where do you start?

- **Get a list of insurance companies** that may cover your services. Your professional organization or state Department of Insurance may be able to provide you with a list of insurance companies, with contact numbers and addresses. Also, *Psychotherapy Finances* has a regular section alerting providers to insurance panel openings, and each year it reports the 25 largest firms nationwide (for *a list of state DOIs, see Page 129. For Psychotherapy* Finances contact information and other resources for lists, see Resources, Page 133).

- **Ask colleagues what provider panels they belong to**, and ask them about their experiences with the plan.

- **Call each insurance company, or go to the plan's Web site to apply.** When calling, ask for the provider relations department. If you are told the network is "closed," this means it is full, or not accepting new providers in your area. But don't take no for an answer. Ask about provider needs, and sell yourself. If you have an unusual specialty, are from a minority culture, lead groups, have a second office, see clients on weekends, or can conduct sessions in another language, let them know — they might make an exception for you.

- **If closed, ask how to apply for future openings.** Find out where to address future correspondence and phone calls, and call back (or e-mail) periodically.

- **Make yourself more attractive (and I don't mean a makeover).** Ask insurers what they are looking for. Consider taking specialized training (such as in substance abuse, crisis intervention, or *Critical Incident Stress Debriefing*), boning up on your Spanish, working a few weekend hours, or renting an office part-time in another geographic area if the plan is saying this might get you on its panel.

> **Tip:** *Eventually, perhaps through attrition, there will be openings on the panel. Submit a letter of interest with a resume by mail or e-mail every three to six months. Try to target your letter to a specific person, or failing this, to "Manager, Network Development" or "Manager, Provider Relations." Follow-up in a week -- try to speak to your targeted person.*

- **Keep a communication log** with dates of your calls, names of the people you spoke with, their responses and action taken.

- **Typically, insurance companies will NOT reimburse interns or associates,** and they may not accept you as a network provider until you have been licensed two to three years. However, I know one intern who found several plans that reimbursed for her work. So ask around. Try smaller and regional plans.

Your Letter of Interest

When applying to a managed care plan, write a letter of interest to include with your resume. Keep it to one page. Be enthusiastic. Think about the following topics before writing your letter, and pick out information that shows you and your skills in the best light. I use bold sections and bullet points in my letter since I know they will be scanning.

- **Specialties/training:** What skills set you apart from colleagues?
- **Brief therapy/crisis intervention:** your training and treatment experience in this.
- **Substance abuse:** your training, assessment, and treatment experience in this area.
- **Managed care experience:** If you belong to other networks, list their names and the number of years of experience as a managed care provider. It demonstrates familiarity with managed care expectations.
- **Location:** Highlight your location's strengths (e.g., close to highways, public transportation, handicap access, location in an underserved area).
- **Availability:** your appointment hours, after-hours availability, etc.
- **Language:** Can you conduct therapy in another language? Sign-language?
- **Ethnic/cultural diversity:** Insurance plans seek therapists of diverse gender, race, ethnicity, and culture. Cross-cultural competency is valued in some areas.
- **Coordination of care:** Tell them if you have hospital privileges or are willing to treat clients just before (or just after) the clients leave the hospital. Let them know if you work closely with your clients' primary care physicians and psychiatrists, and if these doctors will give your clients preferential scheduling.
- **Groups/Classes:** Let them know if you offer therapy/support groups, or psycho-educational classes. You could include a flier from a group you are leading, a brochure from a workshop you are teaching, your practice newsletter, or anything else that will market your uniqueness.

Panel Applications

So you finally find an insurance company that says it is accepting providers, and you are sent an application, or fill one out online. Yippee! Now what will you be asked? It varies with the company, but it may include:

- **Theoretical orientation:** Insurers may ask you to describe your theoretical orientation, often providing a checklist. Most insurance companies are looking for therapists competent in short-term therapy, cognitive-behavioral treatment, and crisis intervention. If you check off only "psychodynamic" or "psychoanalytic," this could put your application on the bottom of the pile – or in the recycle bin.

- **Percentage of cases ended in 5, 10, 15, 20+ sessions:** Again, they are looking for therapists who are comfortable providing short-term treatment, assessment and referral. But don't panic – it is okay to admit that you've seen some clients more than 20 times.

- **Your availability.** Understandably, insurance companies are looking for practitioners who will have enough openings for their members, so they may require that you work at least 20 client hours per week. In addition, many insurance companies use the National Committee for Quality Assurance (NCQA)'s availability standards, looking for therapists who can see routine cases within ten business days, urgent cases within 48 hours, non-life-threatening emergency cases within six hours, and life-threatening emergency cases immediately[11]. And many companies do check up on you by contacting clients to see how long they waited for a first appointment.

- **After-hours/vacation coverage:** Many companies require some form of 24-hour coverage for your clients. They may want your outgoing answering machine message to instruct clients on how to reach you (or a covering therapist) in an emergency or to direct them to go to a nearby emergency room or dial 911.

- **License, malpractice, and CEUs:** Applications typically will ask you to attach a copy of your license, malpractice insurance (they may have certain coverage minimums), and to list your Continuing Education Units from the past few years.

- **Your specialties and certifications.** Don't check off every area on their specialty checklist -- you may lose credibility. Stay within your scope of expertise.

- **Your friends.** They may ask for professional organizations you belong to, psychiatrists you refer to, and colleagues who can vouch for your work.

- **Any history of trouble.** They'll want to know about malpractice claims against you in the last five years, revocations of license, privileges, or professional memberships, and any relevant criminal record. If there is something to report, you may need to submit legal documents to show settlements and dispositions. Be honest. If discovered, lies can lead to big trouble.

- **Your resume.** It's best to prepare a resume targeted for these applications, one that highlights the experience and training you have that insurance companies are looking for. A resume that begins with a summary of these qualifications in bullet form is particularly effective. Keep the resume brief -- one page, if possible. Since insurers are flooded with resumes, don't be afraid to be creative to help yours stand out, but be professional.

- **A release.** Insurers will want you to sign a release to allow them to check out the information you've given them, from schools, malpractice carriers, references, licensing boards, etc.

- **If the application you receive includes a provider contract,** this <u>doesn't</u> mean you have been accepted. *Read it carefully.* While it isn't likely you'll be able to negotiate the terms, reading the contract is the only way you can make an informed decision about whether to join. OK, I know the legal jargon isn't always easy to understand, but you can call the plan with questions. Reading the contract is important because many contracts have special provisions you should know about. For example, one EAP program may allow you to continue privately with a client after the EAP sessions are exhausted, but you must continue to offer the client the discounted fee. Another may state that you cannot continue to see a client after the EAP sessions are over. You'll need to make notes about these different policies so you don't accidently breech the contract, which can put you in hot water.

- **Go over the application thoroughly before submitting.** An application where everything is completed can take four to nine months to be processed. You don't want to leave out any information that could delay the process.

- **Don't leave anything blank.** Write "none" or "N/A" as needed.

- **Keep copies of all applications and letters of interest** in case they are lost.

Another Entry Point: Ad hoc, Temporary, or Single-Case Status

Ad hoc status (also known as temporary or single-case status) means that for one client only, an out-of-network therapist is treated as a network therapist. This is done only in special situations, such as when there is a change of insurance plans during the client's treatment, when there is no therapist with appropriate qualifications available within the network (or within driving distance of the client), or all available professionals have some type of dual role or conflict of interest. It may also be done when the provider is going through the credentialing process. You might be paid at network rates, but you might even be able to negotiate a better rate.

If you are seeing Jack and his insurance changes, and are not a network provider for his new plan, you may be granted a certain number of "transition" sessions by the new plan, or may be allowed to continue with him until the end of that phase of treatment. Usually, a supervisor or provider relations representative will need to approve the request. Unfortunately, such temporary network status rarely becomes permanent, except in cases where you fill a deficit in the network.

It is better to have Jack make a temporary provider request to the insurance plan. But before he does, get a bit of coverage information. Find out if he has out-of-network benefits, and explore the pros and cons of going this route. His cost to see you as an out-of-network therapist may not be much different than seeing a network provider, and he may prefer to go this route instead.

Questions and Answers

What kind of reimbursement can I expect?

Fees vary depending on a variety of factors, including the insurance company, the type of plan, your educational level, and your license. A 2005 subscriber survey by *Psychotherapy Finances* reported the following national averages[12]:

Most Frequent Fees Paid for Individual Therapy
Psychotherapy Finances, Fee and Practice Survey, 2005

	Managed Care	Indemnity Insurance
MFTs	$60	$90
Professional Counselors	$63	$88
Psychologists	$75	$110
Social Workers	$60	$89

Can I negotiate my fee up front before joining?

Good luck. Unless you have something insurers might be willing to pay extra for (e.g., some valuable specialty, skill, language fluency, weekend hours, or if they are in need of providers in your area), it is unlikely they will raise their rates for you, especially before they have had a chance to evaluate your performance.

Can I negotiate anything in the contract?

Provider contracts are fairly standard. The network managers I spoke with told me that except for the occasional raise, most insurance plans won't negotiate any part of their contracts. But it is always worth a try.

How long does it usually take for them to process my application?

It varies greatly between companies, but the wait can be long — sometimes three to nine months.

Once I am accepted, am I in for good?

Insurance companies will require that you go through a recredentialing process about every two or three years, where they recertify that they still want you as part of their network. It's mostly administrative -- they need updated copies of your practice information, license, resume, continuing education, and malpractice insurance. The insurance company's

Recredentialing Committee will also review the information in your provider file, which may include member complaints against you, member satisfaction statistics, length of average client stay, and the results of quality reviews. Some insurers promise to communicate any negative information that may be reported by a third party about you, so that you may review, respond, and correct errors.

While filling out the recredentialing paperwork is a hassle, it's important – if you don't fill it out in a timely manner you may be dropped from the network.

Since therapists often sign contracts with several health plans, the recredentialing paperwork can be a challenge. Health plans are trying to streamline this time-consuming and costly process. Many plans have now contracted with Credentialing Verification Organizations (CVOs), such as CAQH Universal Credentialing DataSource (UCD) or Aperture (see Resources, Page 133). CVOs allow you to complete a single application to meet the credentialing needs of multiple insurance plans. Once you submit your practice data (online or by mail) participating health plans will no longer need to contact you directly with recredentialing forms to seek the necessary information. However, you will still need to update your information with the CVOs, but updating it is fairly simple and quick.

Should I pay a fee to join?

Most companies will not ask for an application fee, but some do. Many therapists I know have paid fees to join a company and never received any clients from that insurance company. Other therapists have paid application fees and received referrals, so they felt it was worth it. If you are considering a network that charges an application fee, ask around to see what other providers' experience has been with that company. *Psychotherapy Finances* also suggests you investigate the company a bit: "Is the company actually providing mental health care coverage to clients, or just printing and distributing a list of providers[13]?"

I have a home office. Is this okay?

Some insurance companies accept home offices, but others (like Blue Cross of California) don't. If they do they will often have certain requirements. The office, client entrance, waiting area, and client restroom may need to be separate from the home living area, used only for business, and you may need to have a dedicated office phone line. United Behavioral Health tells clinicians with home offices that they must also notify clients in advance that the office is in the home, warn of any pets, and offer off-street parking. UBH will not allow high-risk or potentially violent clients to be seen in the home, so telephone screening must be done prior to the first appointment.[14]

6
Talking to the Insurance Company
Who to Talk To and How to Get Through

๛ ๛

How do you know who to call for what? The hierarchy and titles vary with the company, but let's take a minute to review the relevant "cast list" at an average insurance company.

Administrative Staff

- **Provider Relations Representative:** Probably the first person you'll speak with. Deals with all provider-related questions. May handle applications, recredentialing, provider information changes, fee issues, and other administrative duties.

- **Customer Service Representative:** Don't be fooled by the title — these folks can be very helpful to providers. While they are not clinicians, these unsung heroes of the insurance company can handle most non-clinical issues, including answering your basic questions about a client's benefits, coverage, and claims.

- **Claims Representative:** Handles all claims-related issues, such as unpaid claims, underpayments/overpayments, adjustments, and claims denials.

Clinical Staff

- **Intake Worker:** Typically your client's first contact, especially if he or she needs pre-authorization for treatment. The intake worker takes basic clinical information about the presenting problem, assesses for risk factors, helps clients understand their benefits, makes referrals to appropriate network providers, and gives initial authorizations for treatment.

- **Case Manager/Care Manager:** Each client has a case manager, assigned to consider the therapist's requests for additional sessions and handle any clinical issues that arise during treatment. There may instead be a case management team that handles all calls relating to members from a specific company.

- <u>Clinical Director/Medical Director</u>: Advises the case management team on high-risk or difficult cases and proposed denials. Develops treatment policies and guidelines for the company. It is rare that you'd interact with them, except in extreme clinical crises or possibly to request an exception to plan policies.

- <u>Psychiatrist</u>: Provides consultation to case managers, as needed, especially reviewing hospitalizations and proposed denials. Also available to consult with network therapists on their cases.

- <u>Appeals Department:</u> If your request for treatment or claim is denied, and you appeal this decision, these are the folks who will review your appeal.

Navigating the Automated Phone System

It isn't always easy to get through to the right person at an insurance company. In fact, it isn't easy to get thorough to a person at all. But here are some tips to keep in mind:

- **What time is it there?** Make sure you call during normal business hours <u>in the time zone of the insurance company's headquarters.</u> If you are located in on the West Coast, this may mean calling before 1:00 or 2:00 pm. After normal business hours you may reach an answering machine. Even if you reach a live person, the after-hours staff may have limited ability to help you. They are available to assist with clinical emergencies, such as those that require immediate hospital admission.

- **Allow yourself enough time to make the call.** A few minutes between clients is typically not enough to unsnarl a claim or authorization problem. Running out of time and having to call back will only add to your frustration.

- **Before you dial, take a deep breath.** Get all your paperwork together. Be ready to give the client's name, insurance identification number, group number, and date of

birth, as well as your name, phone number, and tax ID number. If you are calling about a claim, know the date(s) of service, and amount you charged.

- **Formulate your question or problem and desired outcome concisely,** so you can be routed to the correct person. Be patient and friendly.

- **Leaving a message?** Leave as much identifying information as possible. This may include your name, phone number with area code (repeated), the client's name (spelled out), the insured's name, plan ID number, client's date of birth, the date(s) of service in question, the charged amount (if it is a claims issue), and details about your problem. If leaving clinical details, be specific. A sample message follows:

"Hi, this is Ima Great LMFT from Crisis Point, California. My number is 408-555-1234. That's 408-555-1234. I'm calling about my client Jack Klutz, K-L-U-T-Z, ID# 167-42-1861, birth date 2/1/61. He was authorized for 12 sessions with me, authorization number 4568473764, and he has only used 10. But I just realized the authorization expires tomorrow. I feel that medical necessity exists to continue treatment, including ongoing depression, anxiety, and sleep disturbance. I don't want to disrupt treatment. Is it possible to get an extension of the expiration date on this authorization until the end of next month? Do you need me to fax you a request for additional sessions? Thanks!"

- **A little self-promotion never hurt.** Always pair your name and the city where you practice. The case manager may remember you next time he or she is looking for a referral in your area.

Tip: **Want to talk to a live person?** If you reach the insurance company's automated service (e.g. "for the status of a submitted claim, press 1, for claims address, press 2"), but would rather speak to someone with a pulse, you can often interrupt and say "Customer Service," "Representative," "Associate," "Agent," or, if all else fails, press "O" or say "Operator" -- <u>even if these options are not mentioned.</u> If this doesn't work, there is one other option: you can do nothing in response to prompts, and you will usually be transferred to a live person (they need to have this for those with rotary phones).

- **Don't take the "fax back" option.** The automated voice may offer to send a "fax back," that is, to fax to you a summary of the client's benefits. Avoid this offer in favor of speaking to a live person. The answers you need are typically not covered in these summaries. Also, the summaries may have only medical coverage information, not mental health, so they can be quite misleading.

- **Both sides should keep a record of the call.** Many insurance companies document all calls, and may even tape record them, which can be good for you if you later need proof they gave you incorrect information. But <u>you</u> should also document the name (first name and last initial) and the direct phone number or extension of each person you speak to, and a record of exactly what they told you.

- **Or forgo the phone altogether.** While I recommend you call when initially checking insurance benefits, a lot of information may be available via the insurance company's Web site (ex. claim status, authorization confirmation, etc.), and you can often e-mail company staff to answer questions not addressed there. For more on what you can do at the company Web site, see Chapter 14.

7
Parity Laws and HIPAA
Laws You Need to Know

ℰ℧ ℭℬ

Just seeing the word "law" or "regulation" might make your eyes glaze over. But here are two laws that many therapists don't know about that may affect how you operate your practice -- and one that can potentially help your clients.

Parity Laws

First, a little history. Prior to parity laws, many health plans either did not cover mental illness at all or provided better coverage for a medical illness. Clients seeking help for mental health issues might have higher co-payments and deductibles and more limited sessions than when they visited their physician for a medical disorder.

How do parity laws help? In some states, parity law requires insurance plans to provide coverage for mental illness treatment that is equal to ("at parity with") the coverage provided for the treatment of other medical illnesses and diseases covered by the plan. This might mean the plan would need to offer the same visit limits, deductibles, and co-payments for mental health sessions as for medical visits.

Do all states have parity laws? Unfortunately, no. Eleven states have no parity laws at all, and in all but five states, parity is limited in some way, typically to certain diagnoses, or to state employees or certain types of plans. Check the chart in Appendix C (Page 137) to see where your state stands on parity laws.

Appendix C says I live in a state where only "Serious Mental Illnesses" (SMI) or "Biologically-Based" disorders are covered. What does that mean? In 25 states, the benefits of parity laws are limited to those with designated diagnoses, often referred to as "Severe Mental Illnesses" (SMI) or "Biologically-Based" Disorders. In these states there are two levels of health coverage: one for clients who have one of the diagnoses listed in the state's parity law, and another level of coverage for clients with "non-parity diagnoses." <u>Because states vary on which diagnoses are considered SMI or "Biologically-Based," you will need to know your state's parity law so you can get the right coverage information when you check a client's insurance.</u>

Example? Let's take the case of Jack, who lives in California, where parity coverage is limited to "Severe Mental Illness." In California only the following diagnoses are considered SMI, and thus afforded parity coverage: Major Depressive Disorder, Bipolar Disorder, Schizoaffective Disorder, Schizophrenia, Bulimia Nervosa, Anorexia Disorder, Panic Disorder, Obsessive-Compulsive Disorder, Autism, and Pervasive Developmental Disorders, as well as Serious Emotional Disturbances of children (SED).

So what if Jack had one of these diagnoses? In many cases, Jack's parity diagnosis may mean a lower co-payment. His deductible (if any) might be lower or even waived. He may be allowed a greater number of sessions per year. In fact, sometimes there is no limit to the number of sessions.

Why do I need to know this? Because when you call the client's insurance, you will need to ask about parity and non-parity benefits. <u>The insurance plan will not always volunteer information about this "higher" level of coverage that comes with a parity diagnosis.</u> This means your clients may have better benefits than they think they have, or better than the ones that are quoted by the plan representative. Many insurance company representatives are unfamiliar with these laws, so the benefits they quote may be for non-parity diagnoses. You may need to patiently explain what you are asking while they look into it. If they don't recognize the word "parity," ask whether there is coverage for Serious Mental Illness (SMI), Severe Emotional Disturbances (SED), or "Biologically-Based" disorders, terms that may be used at their plan or in their state. But as we'll discuss later, not all plans are obligated to follow state parity laws.

How does this affect treatment? Obviously, if Jack is eligible for unlimited sessions, his deductible is waived, and/or the co-payment is minimized due to his parity diagnosis, he may be able to see you more often (and for a longer period of time) than he otherwise could.

Is coverage for a parity diagnosis always better than for a non-parity diagnosis? Surprisingly, no. By definition, parity diagnoses are afforded the same benefit as medical conditions that are covered by the plan. But some clients have better coverage for mental health than for medical. In these cases, a parity diagnosis actually can wind up giving them a reduction in coverage than what they would have for a non-parity diagnosis! The co-payment may be the same (or higher) for mental health as compared to medical, and therapy sessions may be limited if medical benefits are limited. However, this is not usually the case.

Must all insurance companies follow this law? No. Remember, not all states have parity laws, and each state law is different. Also, not all employer groups are governed by state parity laws. The laws do not affect "self-funded" health plans, such as self-insured welfare benefit plans, often sponsored by the largest employers. These self-funded plans are usually entirely exempt from state regulation because they are governed by the federal law known as ERISA (Employee Retirement Income Security Act). State parity laws also do not apply to federally-funded programs or government plans, including the Federal Employees Health Benefit Programs, as they may be governed by federal parity laws. Parity also may not apply to certain plans written outside of the state.

What if a client has a dual diagnosis? If one of the client's diagnoses is parity and one is not, the primary diagnosis billed will be used to determine the level of payment.

Are clients with parity diagnoses exempt from treatment reviews? No. All clients in managed care plans may be subject to treatment reviews by case managers. These clients may actually be more likely to be reviewed, especially if their condition is chronic, their case is complex, progress appears slow or non-existent, and/or treatment is lengthy.

How can I find out more about parity laws in my state? Contact your professional association, your state's Department of Insurance (see Appendix A, Page 129), or the parity resources listed in the Resources List of this manual (see Resources, Page 133).

HIPAA
The Health Insurance Portability and Accountability Act

[Please note: The following section is a general overview of complex regulations that, at this writing, are in the middle of a multi-year phasing-in process. The interpretation of this Act will no doubt evolve over time. For up-to-date information, refer to relevant citations in the Endnotes on Page 125 and the HIPAA section of Resources on Page 133.]

One of the most confusing issues for psychotherapists today is whether they need to comply with HIPAA regulations. HIPAA, which stands for the Health Insurance Portability and Accountability Act, was signed into law in 1996. It was intended to minimize a client's chance of losing health insurance coverage when he or she is no longer covered by an employer's health plan. It also aimed to contain health care costs by streamlining the electronic exchange of client information, to detect and reduce fraud, and to safeguard the confidentiality of a client's private health information. The Act was passed in part because of public concerns about the privacy of medical information, especially in light of the increasing use of computers by insurance plans and medical practices.

HIPAA has four main parts. HIPAA providers need to take steps to "become compliant" in these different areas:

1. **Privacy Standards:** Describes how a client's health information may be used and disclosed, limiting what can be done without a client's knowledge.
2. **Electronic Transaction and Code Set Standards:** These try to create a universal "language" for claims and reimbursement between all insurance payers (ex. diagnosis and procedure codes).
3. **Security Standards:** These guidelines safeguard the client's confidential information from loss, theft, hacking, tampering, etc.
4. **National Identifier Requirement:** This requires all HIPAA providers to have a universal identification number, the National Provider Identifier (NPI), instead of using different provider numbers for each health plan. More about this on Page 36.

Do I have to deal with HIPAA regulations?

Ah, good question. As of this writing there is still some minor disagreement in this area. Many organizations, including the American Psychological Association, suggest that all therapists should consider themselves subject to the regulations of HIPAA[15]. Several health plans have insisted that since their plans are required to be "HIPAA-compliant," the providers they work with must also be. But most industry experts I spoke to agreed that all clinicians could not be forced to follow HIPAA mandates. The experts do agree on one thing: becoming "HIPAA-compliant" is a good idea, since HIPAA may eventually become the standard of care, if not the law, for all clinicians. Soon, insurance claim forms may require a provider's National Provider Identifier. And as our field becomes more electronically dependent, insurance plans are trying to phase out paper claims, and it is likely that plans will eventually refuse to accept paper claims. Also, argues Ofer Zur, a HIPAA expert, "despite the dread and confusion that surrounds HIPAA, at the end of the day HIPAA stands for good, solid psychotherapy practices and low-cost operations[16]."

OK, but do I really have to?

Only HIPAA "covered entities" are required to follow HIPAA's regulations, says David Jensen, staff attorney at the California Association of Marriage and Family Therapists. Who is a covered entity? According to Jensen[17]:

You **DO NOT** have to deal with HIPAA if you exchange all client health data with insurance plans by mail, phone, or fax, not electronically (i.e. via e-mail or Internet). If:

1. You have a self-pay only practice, and don't deal at all with insurance claims, or
2. You give invoices to your clients to submit to their insurance (see sample invoice Page 147), or
3. You bill insurance, but ONLY submit paper claims by mail or fax and you have no one submitting claims electronically on your behalf (such as a billing service or claims clearinghouse).

You **MUST** deal with HIPAA regulations if you exchange any client information with a health plan electronically (via e-mail or Internet), such as:

1. Submitting claims, inquiring about a claim, or receiving a response via e-mail,
2. Inquiring about eligibility, coverage, or benefits, or receiving a response online,
3. Requesting a treatment or referral authorization, or receiving a response online,
4. Receiving an electronic Explanation of Benefits (EOB) or remittance advice
5. Coordinating benefits between multiple insurance plans online, or
6. Having a billing service or claims clearinghouse do any of the above on your behalf.

Remember, says Jensen, "if you call a health plan to get treatment authorized, and the health plan ... responds to your question via the Internet, you have just become a covered entity." If you want to avoid HIPAA, he says, "insist that they use only the phone, the mail, or the fax machine to communicate with you."

I handle administrative details with clients via e-mail, including appointment scheduling, sending statements, online credit card processing, etc. Does this make me a "covered entity?"

No. First of all, HIPAA only applies when you disclose a client's personal health information to a third party. Your client is not a third party. And administrative and billing transactions (such as credit card processing) that do not include the client's private health information are exempt from HIPAA.

Are interns, associates and trainees covered by HIPAA?

Yes. HIPAA applies to all "health care providers," defined as "any person, business, or agency that furnishes bills or receives payment for health care in the normal course of their business."

What about psychotherapy notes? I hear HIPAA requires me to keep two different sets of notes in two different charts.

I put this question to Michael Griffith, staff attorney for the California Association of Marriage and Family Therapists. "HIPAA speaks of two types of notes," he says. "The first is **psychotherapy notes** – a record you may keep of your feelings, thoughts and analysis of sessions, including your counter-transference, ideas, and reactions. HIPAA granted that psychotherapists could keep these notes if they chose, and keep them separately, and not have to release these as part of a client's medical record. The second type of notes is **progress notes**, which are part of the medical record. These are factual notes kept about the sessions (i.e. topics discussed, treatment plans, dates of service, and recommendations made.[18]" Progress notes would also include medications, session start and stop times, the type of service provided, results of clinical tests, diagnoses, prognosis, and progress.

HIPAA affords psychotherapy notes more protection – most notably from insurance plans – than they've been given in the past. Audits or evaluations should not require access to psychotherapy notes.

What does it mean when HIPAA says that psychotherapy notes must be maintained separate from the medical record? "Some lawyers have interpreted HIPAA to say that you may keep both types of notes in the same chart as long as there is some divider. However, it may be wise to keep them in a separate chart," says Griffith. Your psychotherapy notes are notes recorded in any medium, according to HIPAA

OK, so if I'm a "covered entity," what do I need to do?

It's probably easier than you think. While it is not within the scope of this manual to cover all the ins and outs of complying with HIPAA regulations, here are a few things you'll need to do:

1. **Learn about HIPAA and train your employees, if you have any.** Attend a course or read a simple compliance manual.

2. **Give all present and future clients a copy of your "Notice of Privacy Policies."** This is a document that outlines the client's confidentiality rights and limitations as outlined by HIPAA. Most clients don't blink -- they have gotten used to receiving these from their doctors, dentists, and pharmacists. Many professional therapy organizations offer sample copies you can adapt for your practice, or you can get one from any HIPAA course or manual. But remember: <u>You will need to give a copy to ALL your clients from now on, even to self-pay clients</u>. Once you are a HIPAA provider, the policies apply to your entire practice.

3. **Have clients sign an acknowledgement form saying they have received your privacy policy.** Again, a sample form may be available from your professional organization. If the client refuses to sign, document this. To save paperwork, I

simply incorporated the necessary wording into the treatment agreement which I have all new clients sign (more about treatment agreements on Page 44; see also sample treatment agreement Page 145).

- **If clients have objections** about HIPAA privacy policies, provide them with forms where they can express objections and ask for exceptions (again these are available from professional organizations or as part of any HIPAA course or manual).

- **Follow HIPAA security rules.** Provide basic computer security, including virus protection, backup, firewalls, and passwords. Safely shred old confidential records, lock file cabinets and offices, and limit access. If you want to exchange confidential client information by fax, you will need a dedicated fax machine (one that is not used also as a phone line) in an area that is not accessible by unauthorized persons.

- **Apply for a National Provider Identifier, or NPI.** The NPI is a single provider number that replaces the various provider identification numbers that you may have been given by different health plans This number will be unique to you, and used by all health care payers in their communication with you, making claims processing easier and faster. <u>Providers who are covered entities must use the NPI in all transactions by May 23, 2008</u> (some plans may require one sooner), but most insurance companies are encouraging providers to get an NPI before this date. There is no fee to apply. <u>The NPI does not replace the need to use your tax identification number (TIN) or Employer Identification Number (EIN) on claims, as one of these is still required for tax reporting</u> purposes (for more on the EIN, see Page 65).

  While only HIPAA covered entities are required to get a NPI, <u>any health care provider may obtain a NPI:</u> Applying for a NPI does not automatically make you a covered entity. However, one day NPIs may be mandatory. Several health plan representatives I spoke with urged all providers to get one, saying it is likely at some point that they would require all their providers to have a NPI.

  Billing services and clearinghouses should be instructed to use your NPI. Therapists who are employed by clinics, counseling corporations or agencies should use the organization's assigned NPI in one part of the bill, but may also need to get their own for the section that requests the treating provider's NPI (more about this in the discussion on claims in Chapter 11, "Getting Paid")

For more information on HIPAA, and how to apply for an NPI, see Resources on Page 133.

8

Starting Therapy
Checking Coverage and Intake Sessions

ଅ ରଃ

You run a little victory lap around the sand tray when you learn your application has been accepted by CureQuick. Across town, Jack breaks down crying when he sees a pail in the men's room at work, and a coworker urges him to get help. Having dozed through his employer's benefits seminars, he is clueless about his coverage. He pulls out his tattered insurance card, calls CureQuick, and finds out he has mental health coverage as a member of their HMO plan.

First Contact

A typical client entrance into therapy might go like this:

- **Jack gets your name.** How? Perhaps he gets your name from CureQuick, after calling them to request a therapy referral. The intake staff at CureQuick may conduct a brief, structured phone interview with him to determine his needs and location, then give him your name (and possibly a few others). Or Jack may find your name on CureQuick's Web site, where the CureQuick participating provider list is posted. Of course, Jack may also come to you via one of your normal referral sources (colleagues, former clients, friends, his physician, etc.).

- **Jack calls you and sets up an appointment.** <u>I recommend you ask Jack for his insurance information during this phone call</u>. I'll explain why on the next page.

- **If pre-authorization (pre-treatment approval) is required,** Jack will need to notify CureQuick of the appointment and obtain an authorization number. Have him call you back with this number. Why? To ensure he got one. Some plans, including Value Options, do not allow providers to bill clients for a session when a claim is denied by the plan for failure to obtain a required authorization[19].

- **Just "passing through"?** Instead of needing pre-authorization, Jack may have a certain number of "pass-through" sessions per year. This means that without talking to the insurance company he can refer himself into treatment for a certain number of sessions. After this, you would need to contact the insurance company to get approval for further treatment.

- **Not a member of Jack's insurance plan? Don't despair!** Call the plan and check to see if he has coverage for out-of-network providers. In some cases Jack may only have a slightly higher out-of-pocket expense (e.g. a co-payment of $30 instead of $10), and he may be willing to pay this difference if he wants to see you.

Reasons to Contact the Insurance Plan – NOW!

I can't stress enough how important it is to contact a client's insurance company at the beginning of treatment. In fact, I typically do this <u>before</u> the first session. Many therapists do not check a client's insurance, feeling (understandably) that it is the client's responsibility to be familiar with his coverage. It's tempting to let the client handle this, since it is time-consuming, and you may have clients who appear knowledgeable about their insurance benefits. But it only takes a few moments to check their benefits yourself, and if you don't you are increasing the possibility down the line of claim denials, lengthy phone calls to investigate and fight the denial, and therapy bills that clients may be unable to pay.

- **During your first phone contact with Jack,** after setting up an appointment, you might tell him you would like to check his insurance benefits to be sure he has no problem getting reimbursed. Clients are typically thrilled that you are willing to deal with their insurance on their behalf. Then get the necessary insurance information from Jack over the phone (see Page 41 for a form to use when checking coverage).

- **If you don't call now, you may not get paid.** If you don't check coverage up front, it may take months before you find out that your claim was denied, or that charges went toward the client's deductible. This could leave an unpaid balance of hundreds of dollars. Even if your contract allows you to bill Jack, he might be unable to pay, or he may have left your practice, making it hard to collect.

- **Find out if you need an authorization.** Several plans I work with do not allow you to bill the client for sessions where you failed to get authorization.

- **Don't assume.** You may think since you have other Pails "R" Us or CureQuick clients that you already know the coverage details. But coverage depends on which CureQuick plan(s) Pails "R" Us bought for its employees, and which plan Jack chose.

- **Don't trust the information on Jack's insurance card.** Why? See Page 45.

- "But I don't have a release. Doesn't a call to Jack's insurance plan breach confidentiality?" Some therapists worry because the client hasn't really even become a client or signed a release to allow this call. However, this type of communication is typically permitted by law. For example, California Civil Code states that without a release, medical information "may be disclosed to an insurer...or employee benefit plan...to the extent necessary to allow responsibility for payment to be determined and payment to be made[20]."

- "But he already knows his coverage information." Don't rely on your clients, as they are often misinformed or aren't aware of benefit changes that have occurred since they last used their coverage. And after reading this manual you will have a better idea than they will of what questions to ask to determine whether your services will be covered, for how long, and at what rate.

- "Can't I get coverage information by going online?" Many insurance plans have great Web sites that enable you to check benefits, deductibles, and effective dates. But sometimes this information is incomplete, out of date, and may not answer important questions such as parity coverage information, or how much of a deductible has been used so far this year. In addition, when you call, most insurance companies document your call and the information you were given, which could help you to hold them accountable for misquoting benefits if you have reimbursement problems down the line.

- "But I can never reach a live person!" For tips on reaching a breathing human being and navigating the automated phone maze, see Page 28.

- After checking his coverage, call Jack back and clarify what his portion of the payment for the session will be. Remind him to bring this portion of the payment and his insurance card to the first session.

Again, all of this is recommended, not required. You may simply tell Jack that he must check his own insurance benefits, and that he is responsible for paying whatever portion insurance does not cover. But most of the therapists who consult with me after a claim has been denied could have avoided losing money and saved themselves many frustrating phone calls had they only called and asked the right questions before starting treatment.

Checking Benefits

On Page 41, there's a form you can use when you call to check coverage. A few notes:

- "Behavioral health?" Mental health benefits are also known as BEHAVIORAL HEALTH benefits. Be sure to ask for OUTPATIENT MENTAL HEALTH benefits. State this several times during the phone call, as the client's medical benefits may be different. I even initial these words to indicate that I did ask for outpatient mental health benefits during the phone call.

- The insured vs. the client. No matter who your client will be, you will need to get information about the insured. The insured is the policyholder of the plan, usually the employee in an employer-sponsored plan. The client may be the insured if the policy is hers/his. If the client is using the insurance of a spouse, parent, or domestic partner, the spouse, parent, or partner is the insured.

- **50 sessions per year does not always mean 50 sessions.** Remember that a managed care company may not always authorize a client to use all their benefits. It will depend on many factors, especially whether they think there is a "medical necessity" for the sessions (for more about medical necessity, see Chapter 9).

- **Two insurance plans?** Always ask your client if he is covered by more than one insurance plan. If so, you'll want to check his coverage under both plans to see which is the primary plan. See Chapter 17 for more on "double coverage."

- **Deductible used up?** Don't forget to ask how much of the client's deductible has already been used up for the year. It may be that Jack has a $500 deductible, but if he's already used it up for the year, you don't have to worry about it – just collect his co-payment or co-insurance. If he has not used any of it, the first $500 of your therapy charges will have to come out of his pocket. Some plans have separate mental health and medical deductibles. The mental health deductible and session limits may be shared with other mental health providers, such as psychiatrists.

- **When do benefits renew?** While most plans operate on a calendar year, some I have worked with operate on a 12 month calendar, starting July 1 or March 1, or other fiscal year time frames. Why does this matter to you? The deductible and session limits might start again mid-year instead of on New Year's Day.

- **CPT codes: 90847.** Instead of asking the plan if it covers couples/family therapy, ask if this CPT code 90847 is covered, the code for a conjoint or family therapy session from the American Medical Association's Current Procedural Terminology Manual[21] (for more on CPT codes see Page 64, Box 24D, and Resources, Page 133; for more on couples/family therapy, see Page 105).

- **Usual, customary and reasonable fees (UCR).** This applies only to out-of-network providers, and is important unless you collect your full fee up front for the session. UCR is the amount that the insurance company has determined is reasonable for this service, which is based on usual fees for similar providers in your area. Why should you ask about UCRs? It helps to determine exactly what your client should pay you. Let's say your full fee is $100, and Jack has a 20 percent co-insurance, so you collect $20. But CureQuick's UCR is $80 – the maximum they'll allow for this service – which includes Jack's co-insurance. This means you need to charge Jack not only his $20 co-insurance, but the $20 difference between this UCR and your full fee, for a total of $40 per session. Plans won't always tell you their UCR, though it's good to ask. You may have to wait until the claim is processed.

- **Out-of-pocket maximum.** The insurance plan may quote Jack's "out-of-pocket maximum." This is the maximum amount the client is required to pay "out of his pocket" before his insurance begins to pay 100 percent of covered expenses. However, since these numbers are typically quite high, in most cases this is not benefit information you will need to know, so it is not on my chart.

- **Is the information I get a guarantee of coverage?** No. There are lots of reasons why information the plan gives you may be incorrect. Be sure clients understand (and agree in writing) that they are responsible for any portion unpaid by the plan (see treatment agreements, Page 44, and sample agreement, Page 145).

CHECKING COVERAGE: 12 ESSENTIAL QUESTIONS

BEFORE CALLING INSURANCE: INFO TO GET FROM THE CLIENT

1. Client: _____ ID #:_____
2. Insured (if other): _____ ID #:_____
3. Relationship: _____ Group/Account Number: _____
4. Insured's Date of Birth:____ /____ /____ Client's Date of Birth: __ /__ /__
5. Insured's Employer_____
6. Insurance Phone Number (May say "MH/SA Benefits," "Eligibility and Benefits," "For Pre-Authorization," "Customer Service"): _____

THE CALL: WHAT TO ASK THE INSURANCE COMPANY

CALL DATE: __ /__ /__ REPRESENTATIVE SPOKEN TO: _____

Request "outpatient mental health benefits." Tell them if you are a network provider.

	Non-Parity Diagnosis	Parity Diagnosis (SMI, Biologically-Based)
1. Co-payment (flat fee) or Co-insurance (percent)		
2. Deductible (if applicable)		
3. Sessions Allowed per year		
4. Effective Date of Coverage	_____/_____/_____	
5. When Do Benefits Renew?	_____/_____/_____	
6. Deductible met this year	$_____._____	
7. Is Pre-authorization Needed?	Yes _____ No _____ • If Yes: Auth #:_____ • # of Sessions Authorized:_____ • Starts:__ /__ /____ Expires:__ /__ /____	
8. Claim: Use new CMS-1500?	Yes _____ No _____	
9. Claims address for MENTAL HEALTH claims		
10. Is CPT code 90847 (couples/family) covered?	Yes _____ No _____	
Out-of- Network Providers: 11. Is my license covered?	Yes _____ No _____	
12. What is the UCR (usual, customary, reasonable fee)?	$_____	

Translating "Insurance-Speak"

Now for a quiz to see if you can interpret the language of insurance representatives.

For this example, let's say that you have signed a contract with Jack's insurance plan, CureQuick, to see their members at a fee of $67 per session. This is your "contracted rate."

What the Representative Tells You	What Jack Will Have To Pay	What Insurance Will Pay
"He has a $10 co-payment after which he is covered at 100 percent."	Jack will pay $10 (his co-payment) per session.	$57. To calculate, take your contracted rate of $67, and subtract Jack's co-payment of $10
"Jack is covered at 70 percent."	Jack must pay 30 percent of your contracted rate of $67, a total of $20.10 per session.	$46.90 (70 percent of the contracted rate of $67)
"Jack is covered at 90 percent, up to a maximum of $25 per session."	You can go ahead and figure out what 90 percent of your contracted rate is ($60.30), but the rep is telling you that the most CureQuick will pay per session is $25. Jack pays the difference between the $25 insurance reimbursement and the contracted rate of $67, which is $42.	$25
"Jack has a deductible of $150, and none of it has been used. After that he is covered at 90 percent.	Here things get interesting. All of Sessions 1 and 2 will go toward the deductible, so Jack will pay $67 for each session, using up $134 of the deductible. In Session 3, Jack must pay $16 of your $67 fee to finish the deductible, plus 10 percent of the remaining $51 ($16 + $5.10 = $21.10). After this he will pay 10 percent of your contracted rate, or $6.70 per session.	For Session 1 and 2, insurance pays $0. For Session 3, the plan pays $45.90 ($67 minus Jack's co-pay of $21.10). After this, the plan pays at 90 percent of $67, or $60.30 per session.

Care Denials: Bad News before Treatment Begins

When you call to check Jack's coverage, CureQuick may tell you it does not cover the services Jack is seeking. Common reasons might be:

- **Jack has used up his insurance benefits for the year** with other providers.

- **Jack is no longer (or not yet) covered by the health plan.** He may have recently left his job or started a new one. There is sometimes a gap between when a client gets a new job and when his insurance "kicks in." Another good reason for checking benefits at the start of treatment!

- **The service you intend to provide is not a covered benefit.** Not all insurance companies, for example, cover less traditional therapies such as Eye Movement Desensitization and Reprocessing (EMDR) or hypnosis. You may also be refused if it is not clear that a diagnosed mental disorder is being treated.

- **The insurer doesn't cover "couples counseling."** If you want to see Jack and Jill together, remember that insurance will typically cover couples counseling only when used to address a diagnosable mental illness. To bill a plan for couples therapy, you must be prepared to assert that one member of the couple has a diagnosis (typically a V-code alone is not enough, though one therapist I know says she has been reimbursed for this). But remember: It is insurance fraud to overstate or create a diagnosis for the purpose of ensuring reimbursement. In addition, you will have to make the case that couples counseling is the most effective means to treat your client. For more on couples counseling, see Chapter 17.

- **The plan is a self-insured welfare benefit plan, ERISA plan, or for some other reason doesn't cover providers with your license.** Some plans are "self-insured" or "self-funded." This means that instead of purchasing a pre-packaged plan from an insurance company, the employer has set aside monies to pay for a plan which may be specially designed for its employees. These plans are governed by ERISA (Employee Retirement Income Security Act), a federal law. The problem is that the states have no jurisdiction for employees covered by self-funded plans. ERISA preempts state law, including state "Freedom of Choice" laws which allow clients a choice of providers with a wider variety of licenses. For example, this might mean that an ERISA plan might not cover the client's visits to a Licensed Marriage and Family Therapist. <u>However, don't assume: this is not always an issue with ERISA plans.</u>

- **The plan is an "out-of-state" plan,** where the insurance was written for delivery in another state. This may be the case if the client is vacationing or temporarily working in your state, or if the employer is headquartered in another state. In this case they are not governed by your state's "Freedom of Choice" laws and thus may not recognize your license as an authorized provider. However, don't assume that because the insurance company has an out-of-state address you are in trouble. Even if denied, you may be successful if you appeal.

And what if you are denied? Don't be discouraged. Care denials can often be overturned if you know how to approach the relevant issues (see Chapter 13 for a wealth of ideas).

The First Session

In the first session, take a bit of time to educate Jack about what it means if he chooses to use his insurance. After reading this manual, hopefully you'll be able to communicate with all your clients about the pros and cons of using insurance, and about confidentiality issues and coverage limitations, so they can make informed choices. Many professional organizations offer a brochure you can give clients on the use of insurance in therapy.

If this is an EAP session, go over Jack's EAP benefit with him. Explain your role is to assess his situation and determine if it can be resolved within the specified number of sessions or if longer-term counseling and/or a referral is needed. Also let him know about other free assistance that may be available to him via his EAP, such as legal and financial consultations, and referrals for child and elder care.

Reasons for a Treatment Agreement

While giving clients a treatment agreement is not legally mandated, I highly recommend that you give one to all new clients. This agreement (which they will sign) is a form that educates them about how your practice operates, including your fees, the length of sessions, how payment and billing will be handled, the limits of confidentiality, your cancellation policy, termination, and after-hours coverage. It can also be used to inform clients about your insurance policies (see the Sample Treatment Agreement on Page 145). Some sentences that you can adapt to fit your policies might include:

- "The client is responsible for verifying and understanding the limits of his/her insurance coverage, as well as for any co-payments and deductibles."

- "The client is responsible for any and all fees not reimbursed by the insurance plan."

- Either "the therapist is a contracted provider with _____ insurance plan, and has agreed to a specified fee, and will bill the plan on the client's behalf" or "the therapist is <u>not</u> a contracted provider with the client's insurance plan. Should the client choose to bill insurance, the therapist will provide the client with a statement of fees paid at the time of the session, to submit to the plan for reimbursement."

- "The client must pay all insurance co-payments and deductibles, if applicable, at the time of the session."

- "If the client misses a session or cancels without 24-hour notice, he/she is responsible for paying the therapist's missed session fee of $_____ (not just the insurance co-payment). Insurance plans typically will not reimburse for missed sessions."

- "By signing this form, the client authorizes the release of any information needed to process insurance or EAP claims, to request additional sessions, to verify medical necessity of the sessions, or to satisfy the insurance plan's audits or quality reviews."

- "By signing below, the client authorizes insurance payments be made to the therapist" (*omit this if your clients will be paying you in full and billing insurance themselves*).

- "By signing, you acknowledge receipt of the Notice of Privacy Practices, as required by HIPAA" (*note: include this only if you are a HIPAA "covered entity" – more on this in Chapter 7*).

The Insurance Card – And Why You Shouldn't Trust It

PAILS "R" US

CureQuick
Behavioral Health
www.curequick.com   Wonderful Optima HMO

GROUP: 23560   Deductible: $0
                                     Office co-payment: $10
MEMBER ID: PRU34567   Specialist: $25

JACK ISA KLUTZ

Plan 040: Wellquick Pharmacy – Medical

This card does not prove membership nor guarantee coverage. For verification of benefits, please call Customer Service.

Providers: For self service, go to www.curequick.com
Or call Customer Service: 1-800-555-3975

Claims: P.O Box 533, SUMMIT, N.J. 07901

For MH/SA benefits, call 1-800-279-5555

In the first session, copy both sides of Jack's insurance card, and keep a copy in his chart. Look for the phone number to call for mental health benefits. It might say "for Eligibility and Benefits" or simply "Customer Service." In Jack's case, you will see the back of his card has two phone numbers. The one you want is labeled "for MH/SA," which means "for mental health and substance abuse benefits."

So why shouldn't I trust insurance cards?

- **The information may not apply to you.** Often, as in Jack's case, the deductible and co-payment information you see printed on the front of the card applies to medical services, not mental health.

- **The claims address may not apply to you.** Often, as In Jack's case, the claims address is for medical claims, not mental health, and the mental health claims address is not even printed on the card. Do not assume the claims address is the same as CureQuick's corporate address, or the address where you mail other information.

Even the name of the insurance company on the card might be irrelevant. Often mental health services have been "carved out." This means CureQuick may manage its members' medical claims, but may have hired another company to manage mental health benefits. Why is this important to you? I was once fooled when a client told me she had benefits with CIGNA Health Plan (for which I am a network provider), but I later found out her mental health benefits were handled by another plan, in which I was not a network provider. This is another reason to call the insurance before the client comes for the first session. Of course, this can work the other way: clients who tell me they have Aetna (of which I am not a provider) may turn out to have mental health provided by CIGNA, so I will be covered.

9
Getting More Sessions
Authorization Requests

ဆၠ ဢ

So you've been working with Jack for some time, and of course he is improving with your expert care. However, while he is functioning better, he continues to have intrusive anxiety symptoms and sleep problems. He'd like to continue working with you to eliminate these symptoms. You notice he is almost out of authorized sessions.

Managed care companies perform treatment reviews in order to monitor both the quality of the care you are providing and the clinical need for continued care.

The need to request more sessions after treatment has begun usually applies only for your HMO clients, and some EPO and POS clients. PPO clients typically don't require authorization of sessions. And you won't usually request additional sessions with EAP clients, as the client usually is allotted the maximum number of sessions up front.

While some companies allow you to call to request more sessions (some plans even have automated phone request systems), you may need to fill out a request form provided by the insurance company, sometimes called the Outpatient Treatment Report (OTR) or Request for Reauthorization (RFR). This form can often be faxed to the insurance plan or filled out online at the company's Web site for the fastest response. If approved, you will usually receive an authorization in the mail or by fax within two weeks of your submission. If you don't receive the form, contact the insurance company again.

What will they ask? Using a checklist and/or a narrative format, the insurance company may ask how treatment is progressing, your diagnosis, what symptoms the client is currently experiencing, why you feel there is a need for ongoing treatment, your treatment goals, and planned interventions for the next phase of therapy.

Who reviews the authorization requests? Susan Frager, a former case manager, writes that "because of the high volume of treatment reports received by the managed care companies, it's cheaper to pay associates with a bachelor's degree, or unlicensed master's degree, to handle the majority of the load (or have a computer do it) than it is to pay fully-licensed, experienced clinicians. Under this system, the complex reports and/or the ones in which there is a question of denial are weeded out and sent to a licensed clinician for review[22]." The rest are certified by the associates. "Case managers focus their efforts only on cases where the patient is not progressing, where utilization is higher than average, or on patients with chronic, severe conditions that need careful management to avoid multiple hospitalizations," she says.

How often do I have to request more sessions?

This depends on the insurance company and plan. I have seen a strong movement away from the use of this type of session management and paperwork on every case – it is too time-consuming and expensive for the insurance plans to manage. Many plans have switched to allotting the full amount of yearly sessions when the client first calls for treatment, so you shouldn't have to get more sessions all year. However, there are still some health plans that only give out five or six sessions at a time. If you are seeing a client weekly, you would need to submit a new treatment request every five to six weeks. If you are seeing the client every other week, you would only have to submit one every 10 to 12 weeks. Other companies give 10 to 20 sessions each time, so you may only need to submit one every two to four months.

How early do I have to submit these requests?

Submit these requests at least two weeks before the expiration date of the previous authorization or at least two weeks before you need the new one. Thus if Jack has an authorization for 10 sessions expiring February 1, it is a good idea to submit it around Session 8 (if you are meeting weekly) or January 19, whichever comes first. I would recommend two weeks even if filing online or via fax -- the earlier the better. If your request for more sessions is refused, you might need time to end with the client and refer, if needed. Keep copies of all completed authorization requests (even those submitted online) in the client's chart.

What Case Mangers Look For: "Medical Necessity"

Health insurance contracts are written for the purpose of covering sickness and illness. Therefore, the managed care company staff member who is reviewing your authorization request will be looking for the **"medical necessity"** of treatment. This means that he or she must be convinced that a psychiatric condition or illness is being treated, and that the treatment is medically necessary to treat the symptoms or illness.

What does this really mean? While medical necessity criteria vary between insurance plans, here are some common components that can give us a clue about what the folks at CureQuick might be looking for when they look over your request for sessions:

- **Medical symptoms.** Jack's treatment must alleviate some medical symptoms (such as anxiety or depression). The focus of treatment typically cannot simply be "growth-oriented" or targeting poor self-esteem, inadequate communication skills, an annoying spouse, or parenting issues. That is, the client usually needs more than a V-Code diagnosis. When listing a diagnosis, the plan may require that the diagnosis be one listed in the American Medical Association's most recent ICD, or *International Classification of Diseases* (see Resources, Page 133)[23]. Many psychotherapists use the American Psychiatric Association's DSM, or *Diagnostic and Statistical Manual of Mental Disorders*[24]. But don't worry: Newer versions of the DSM have the same coding as the ICD. In spite of this, I recommend you get the latest ICD list from your professional organization or the American Medical

Association. The most important thing to remember: use the <u>maximum</u> number of digits the diagnosis requires (3, 4, or 5 digits, depending on the diagnosis).

- **A decrease in functioning.** Presenting symptoms must have led to a decrease in Jack's pre-illness or baseline level of functioning.

- **The service is deemed appropriate** and within accepted standards of care for the symptoms, diagnosis, or treatment of Jack's condition. It is believed to be the most appropriate type, level, and length of treatment needed. And it isn't primarily for Jack's convenience (or yours).

- **The client is engaged in treatment.** Jack must be motivated and participating in treatment, attending sessions and following recommendations.

- **The treatment is working.** Jack is receiving some measurable benefit and making progress. The CureQuick staff will be comparing his current functioning to his pre-therapy level. At the very least, they must feel you are stabilizing the client enough to prevent hospitalization.

- **The problem seems resolvable.** If CureQuick feels that it has paid for too much therapy without improvement, they may conclude Jack's problem cannot be resolved in outpatient therapy. Clients who have reached therapeutic plateaus may be considered more appropriate for referral to community support groups for maintenance. This places those with chronic conditions, including the severely mentally ill, in danger of eventual denial.

- **About the GAF score.** While medical necessity criteria varies, several insurance companies look for a GAF (Global Assessment of Functioning) score from the *APA's Diagnostic and Statistical Manual of Mental Disorders* that is above 40 and below 69 for outpatient therapy[25]. Why? The plan may feel outpatient treatment is not appropriate for a GAF that is too low, and may not see the medical necessity for treatment if the GAF is too high.

- **Work with kids requires work with family.** When working with a child or adolescent, your treatment plan typically must include some family therapy.

In addition, those evaluating your requests will check for potential risk issues, such as suicidal and homicidal ideation, chemical dependency, domestic violence, or abuse issues.

Writing a Treatment Update

Reading lengthy treatment reviews is time-consuming and thus costly to the managed care company. Therefore, the trend seems to be away from asking for a narrative summary of treatment, preferring the more quickly-read checklists. But in case you are asked to write a narrative summary with interventions and goals, here is an example that might give you some pointers:

**Progress Summary:** _Insomnia has decreased from daily to twice weekly. Client continues to have nightmares and flashbacks of moderate intensity twice weekly. While overall anxiety has decreased, client continues to experience periods of heightened anxiety when near pails, including heart racing and sweaty palms, and an exaggerated startle response. Because his job involves exposure to pails, he is on restricted duty at work, which has put a financial strain on family. He feels irritable, has withdrawn from others, and shows a restricted range of affect._

**Interventions:** _Help client develop self-soothing skills. Teach relaxation, meditation, cognitive reframing, and visualization techniques. Teach client to identify cognitions and coping mechanisms (such as avoidance) that increase anxiety. Assign exercises from anxiety workbook. Encourage client to journal, exercise, and/or call friends when anxious. Monitor adherence to medication regime and follow-up visits with psychiatrist._

**Goals:** _Client will report insomnia, nightmares and flashbacks not more than once per week, and of lesser intensity. Periods of intense anxiety will be less frequent and of shorter duration. Client will demonstrate lower scores on anxiety checklist. Client will take medications as prescribed, and will get watch alarm to remind him to take medication faithfully. Client will take daily walks, and report practicing relaxation and coping techniques at least once daily._

Authorization Requests: Dos and Don'ts

Do:

- **Focus on symptoms, and be specific.** Remember, this is the medical model, so communicate in this language. List the symptoms the client is experiencing that have led to a decrease in his or her usual level of functioning. Replace casual language such as "stressed" with specific clinical symptoms, severity and frequency, and scores on diagnostic tests. Include how the diagnosis has affected his "activities of daily living" (ADLs) such as work, family, friendships, finances, self-care, etc. Focus on current symptoms that support the diagnosis, and avoid irrelevant details.

- **Address how treatment will reduce impairment.** How will it reduce symptoms? And how do the sessions avoid the need for more intensive/expensive care? Remember, cost containment is one of the goals of a managed care company, so keep this in mind when conversing with case managers.

- **If asked about your goals,** make sure they are clear, measurable, realistic, and consistent with the presenting problem and diagnosis. Identify how you will know if the desired change has taken place. As in the narrative example above, try to quantify treatment goals.

- **Explain your interventions** (what you plan to do to help the client achieve the goals). Again, see the example above. Avoid sentences such as "help Jack identify feelings about accident" in favor or more symptom-oriented statements.

- **Don't be afraid to say if the client is doing worse.** However, explain this, if possible, and identify any new problems that have come up since treatment began.

50

Try to identify any areas of progress you see, however small. Case managers understand that progress isn't always linear and smooth.

- **Document any referrals for medication evaluation.** With clients who have a major affective disorder, a referral for medications should be discussed. Document this discussion, and referrals made, even if the client refuses to follow-up.

- **Document your referrals to community resources.** Document referrals to 12-Step programs, treatment facilities, anger management classes or support groups, even if refused.

- **Document a safety plan** when the client is a danger to self or others or gravely disabled.

Don't:

- **Don't be vague.** Case managers report they are likely to remember the names of therapists who turn in poor treatment plans, which lack specific goals and outcome or progress criteria. Vague treatment goals may lead the care manager to authorize only one or two sessions while the therapist is asked to fill out a new treatment request or schedule a phone interview. More work for you.

- **Don't try to solve all the client's problems.** Identify goals that can realistically be achieved within six to nine months.

- **Avoid aiming for symptom elimination.** Remember that managed care companies may not feel they need to continue to cover a client until the symptoms have vanished. In some cases, returning the client to baseline functioning -- or stabilizing and referring to community support -- may be all they will cover.

- **Avoid clinical speculation.** Don't speculate about why a client acts as he does. Your clinical theory is not particularly relevant.

- **Don't dwell on the past.** Don't bring up the client's past, unless it is extremely relevant and directly impacts the client's present impairment. Even then, keep it brief. Stay focused on current symptoms.

- **Don't just list stressors.** The fact that a client is going through a divorce does not give the case manager enough information to understand the symptoms that this particular client is experiencing.

- **Don't list "poor self-esteem" as the sole reason for treatment.** "Saying a client has low self-esteem is the kiss of death," says former case manager Norman Hering. "Managed care companies don't see low self-esteem as 'medically necessary[26].'"

- **Don't reveal any more information than you must.** Make every effort to protect a client's confidential health information. In cases where you feel you need to disclose very sensitive information in order to get more sessions, discuss this with the client (and document the conversation) so he can make an informed choice. He may decide he would rather pay out of pocket than reveal this information.

- **Don't just resubmit a copy of your last authorization request,** even if little has changed. The lack of new information may trigger a case manager's review.

It sometimes happens that your client no longer meets the criteria for medical necessity, yet you still feel the client needs ongoing care to address underlying or chronic issues. You may be concerned that these issues, if left untreated, could result in a regression of the client's symptoms. A client with a history of recurrent depression, a background of childhood abuse, or with perpetual problems with intimacy in relationships could fall into this category. If your client no longer meets the criteria for medical necessity, you could argue for the need for maintenance sessions to prevent relapse, request more sessions to do discharge planning, refer the client, or contract with the client to pay out of pocket.

Why Your Request Might Get a Closer Look

Let's look at some of the reasons why your request for more sessions might get a closer examination or outright denial:

- **It's incomplete, illegible, or so vague** it is worthless.

- **It is a copy of the request you sent last time.**

- **Your diagnosis doesn't match the symptoms reported.**
- **You are ignoring a potential substance abuse issue.** You haven't assessed for this, or if you have diagnosed a drug or alcohol problem, you didn't refer Jack to a treatment program or to a 12-Step program.

- **There is no medication evaluation.** You have diagnosed Jack as having Major Depression or Bipolar Disorder, but he is not on medications, and you have not referred him for a medication evaluation or explained why you did not make such a referral.

- **You deferred the diagnosis.** You need to give a working diagnosis. You can always change it later as your assessment continues, if needed.

- **You did not include a complete five Axis diagnosis, if requested, or did not include all the modifiers, if any.** Modifiers are the digits found to the right of the decimal point in diagnosis codes. The case manager needs to enter a full diagnosis into the computer. Remember that most – but not all -- diagnoses need two digits to the right of the decimal point.

- **If you're asking to see Jack several times a week, if you've used a lot of sessions, or if Jack seems highly impaired,** the case manager may question why Jack is not in a higher level of care. But don't be defensive. "Questions from the case manager regarding whether a client needs more intensive treatment are generally not a reflection of the case manager's opinion of the therapist's abilities," former case manager Susan Frager explains[27]. "If the client's benefit plan only allows 20 outpatient sessions per year, twice weekly therapy will use a year's worth of benefits in two and a half months. Part of the case manager's job...is to consider whether another level of care would be more effective at helping the client reach the same treatment goals while conserving limited benefits."

- **Axis II diagnosis.** If Jack has a personality disorder, it may be questioned whether he can benefit from short-term, symptom-reduction therapy. Your treatment goals need to be especially realistic, and your case may undergo closer review.

- **You're an ad hoc provider or your clients have complained.** In these situations, your treatment reports may get additional scrutiny.

- **There are no more sessions available.** Jack has used the maximum number of sessions available to him this year, so the case manager has no more to give.

- **No progress.** You've worked with Jack for some time with no improvement. The insurance company may consider discontinuing, or conclude that a different level or type of treatment is necessary.

- **Great progress.** If Jack's symptoms are mild and his GAF score is high, the insurance company may conclude that treatment is no longer medically necessary, and Jack is well enough to leave your care.

As you can see, continued treatment requires the picture of a client who is not too healthy or, conversely, too ill!

Questions and Answers

What if Jack plans to use his insurance plan, but in our initial session it becomes clear to me that he does not meet the criteria for medical necessity?

Good question. A truly ethical therapist would explain to Jack that while he may be able to benefit from therapy, from what he has said thus far you do not have evidence that he has a mental illness that would be covered by his health insurance. You might also explain that it would be insurance fraud to make up a diagnosis just so that he is covered, and that doing so could place your license in jeopardy. You might also explain that this could be good news for him, as he will not have a diagnosis in your records that could cause problems for him down the line. You may want to call Jack's health plan to check if they will cover this initial assessment session, and if they might cover a V-code diagnosis, if he has one of these. You could offer to see him in your practice to work on his presenting problems, but be clear that he would need to pay out of his pocket. Of course, you should allow him adequate advance notice of this situation so he has time to consider his options.

Let's say I have been treating Jack for many months, and he improves to the point that I no longer feel he meets the criteria for medical necessity. What then?

Another great question. If you are merely wanting a few more sessions before ending with Jack to make sure he is stable and does not relapse, it could be argued that this is part of your medically necessary treatment. However, if you are continuing merely because Jack likes coming, or if the focus of treatment is general relationship or personal growth issues and <u>not</u> a mental illness, this is a different story. You would want to congratulate Jack on his progress, and explain to him you feel he has improved to the point that he no longer has a diagnosis that is covered by his health plan. While he might benefit from continued therapy, he would need to pay for future sessions out of his pocket. Again, give him advance notice so that this discussion does not leave Jack feeling abandoned.

Retro-authorizations and Extensions

"Yikes! "I just realized I've seen Jack six times, and he only had an authorization for five sessions!"

"Aiyee! I just realized Jack's authorization expired last week, and I've seen him once since then!"

Being a managed care provider takes a bit of organization, and sometimes we overlook an important deadline, or something slips between the cracks. This may lead to sudden realizations, and a certain amount of accompanying hair-pulling.

But don't panic. Case managers get these calls daily. While it is possible that they might say they can't help you, in most cases they will "retro-authorize" these sessions. This means that an authorization is issued after the fact and back-dated to cover a session that has already taken place. Many plans have a limit to how far back they can back-date an authorization, so call as soon as you notice.

What do you say when you call to talk to the case manager about this situation? See the sample script in the section on "Navigating the Automated Phone System," Page 28. Use a friendly but professional tone. Take responsibility for your error, but demonstrate that your primary concern is making sure your client's treatment is not affected due to your clerical error. Outline the medical necessity for any sessions that were not previously authorized (or occurred after the expiration date), and document the conversation.

If the case manager refuses, you can always appeal (a sample appeal letter requesting retro-authorization can be found on Page 84). You may want to call the clinical director or medical director, especially in cases where you are asking for a policy exception.

In both of the examples above, you'll note that even if the company agrees to retro-authorize the last session, the client has no more authorized sessions. You will need to quickly submit a treatment update or reauthorization request.

10
Ongoing Therapy
ഇൻ ൙

So Jack has been coming to see you, and naturally, is progressing amazingly under your excellent treatment!

Feel free to pat yourself on the back! But here are a few things to keep in mind as you continue to work with him:

- **Be aware of your client's benefits.** Jack may get ten sessions that expire six months from the start of therapy, or every calendar year, or every fiscal year. This may make a difference in how you space sessions.

- **Keep track of the number of authorized sessions remaining,** and the authorization's expiration date.

- **Deductible details.** As was explained in Chapter 2, if you are a network provider and Jack has a deductible, you collect your contracted rate for each session until the deductible is satisfied. You still need to submit the bill to Jack's insurance (or have Jack submit it) for these sessions so that his payments will be counted toward his deductible; otherwise, the insurance company will not be aware that he has met his deductible

- **New Year?** If Jack has a deductible, you'll typically need to collect it in the first sessions of the New Year. But don't assume you know how much it is. <u>When Jack's benefits renew, usually January 1, call his insurance plan!</u> It's a hassle, but it's worth it to avoid later problems. Jack may have a new plan, or his plan may have a new benefit structure. Here's an all-too-common scenario: Jack is unaware his deductible has gone up from $150 to $300, and his co-payment increased from $10 to $25. By the time your January claims are processed and returned to you, Jack may owe you over $250. He may even have discontinued therapy, making it harder to collect.

- **Document changes in diagnosis.** As treatment progresses you might reconsider your initial diagnosis, or the client's symptoms may change. Be sure to document your new diagnosis (and the symptoms that led to it) in the client's chart, and change it on future claim forms.

- **Job changes may mean coverage changes.** If Jack leaves or loses his job, be sure to check for changes in (or loss of) insurance coverage.

- **Insurance authorizations are often flexible.** As was suggested in the previous chapter, you can often get case managers to extend the expiration date on an authorization if your client hasn't used all his allotted sessions. For example, if Jack has been given eight sessions to see you, and has only used six of those by the authorization's December 28 expiration date, it usually only involves a simple phone call to have the insurance company extend the expiration date.

- **Don't keep the doctor away.** Keep the primary care physician, psychiatrist, and all other treating health professionals in the loop. Most insurance companies want you to get a signed release from your client to contact his doctor. If he refuses, the reason should be documented in your notes. This is especially important if the client has a significant health issue, has substance abuse issues (or a history of addiction), or is taking psychiatric medications. Additional contact is recommended when the client is unstable, at risk, or when there are significant changes in the client's condition.

- **If you need to refer Jack to another provider,** such as a doctor, a psychiatrist, a psychiatric hospital program or substance abuse treatment program, contact the insurance company for referrals within his plan. You or your client might also check the plan's Web site for a network provider list. Remember that the client may need pre-authorization for this care, especially for inpatient or structured outpatient programs.

Losing Coverage

When a client goes through a major life change like divorce or the loss of a job, the possibility of losing health insurance coverage may be the last thing on his mind. But it should be on yours, as losing coverage could impact therapy.

If your client loses his group coverage, in certain situations (such as when a company changes health plans) the new insurance plan may pay for you to have a certain number of transitional sessions with the client, to allow the client time to terminate or to transition to a provider in his new network. You might consider using this time to apply to become a provider in the client's new health plan, or to explain to the client the option of contacting his employer's human resources department or benefit administrator to express concerns about the lack of continuity of care.

The client, of course, may choose to continue to see you, paying out of pocket. In this case, have him sign a self-pay agreement (such as the one on Page 151), documenting that he understands there has been a change in the payment agreement.

You might also ask your client if he is eligible for COBRA coverage. COBRA (Consolidated Omnibus Budget Reconciliation Act) is a federal statute that requires employers to offer employees and dependents who would otherwise lose their insurance the opportunity to purchase the same coverage the employer provides to its employees. COBRA is available for clients who lost coverage when they were fired, quit their jobs, had work hours cut to a level that they lost their eligibility for coverage, became disabled, divorced, lost their dependent child status, or when the employee died. If Jack lost his job at Pails "R" Us, and was in danger of losing his CureQuick coverage, he could apply for COBRA. This would entitle him to continue with the same coverage he had while employed, but he would take over payment of the premium (the monthly or yearly cost paid to receive the insurance coverage). No physical exam is required. But he must act fast to sign up so there is no break in coverage (breaks can jeopardize the ability to get later coverage). There are also limits to this continuation of coverage (usually 18 months for loss of employment or work hour reduction, 29 months for disability-related events, or 36 months for dependents who would lose coverage for reasons other than employment loss by the employee).

If your client switches to COBRA coverage, what does this mean for you? If the client submitted his COBRA application in a timely fashion (you might want to get proof of this) and it was processed smoothly, not much changes in your therapy. You keep submitting claims, and the plan continues to pay, as if nothing had changed, since all that has changed is who is paying the premium.

If your client has exhausted COBRA benefits, he may then be eligible for HIPAA individual coverage or an individual conversion coverage plan (offered by the same plan that provided the client's group coverage). For details about these plans and other health plans for clients in this position contact your state's Department of Insurance or Department of Managed Care (see Appendix A, Page 129) or the U.S. Uninsured Helpline (see Resources, Page 133).

Questions and Answers

Will a case manager ever call to discuss a case?

Again, this depends on the insurance company, how much work you do with managed care, and the difficulty of the cases you happen to have. You may never be called. Even with my high caseload, I am called by a case manager only about once a year. One insurance company representative told me that while her company had done away with the authorization request process, they still contact providers occasionally to check on progress, especially in cases where treatment had significantly exceeded what would be expected for the diagnosis.

What if my client has used up all his sessions for the year? Is there any possibility I could get more if I felt it was absolutely necessary?

If the insurance company is convinced the client is best served by ongoing treatment with you, they may get creative to assist the client in getting this care. Two insurance insiders told me that at times a case manager might approve a "trade" or "exchange of benefits." For example, if the client has 30 days of coverage per year for inpatient psychiatric hospitalization, the client and insurance company might be willing to trade some of those days (reducing the inpatient benefit) in exchange for additional days of outpatient therapy with you (increasing the outpatient benefit) in order to prevent a hospitalization. As you might imagine, this is a cost savings for them – exchanging one day in a hospital for one hour of outpatient treatment.

What happens if a client complains about me to the health plan?

It is always in your best interest to take the pro-active approach and call the insurance company if you suspect a member is unhappy with you. If the member files a complaint, you will be contacted for a response, a request may be made for copies of medical records and other supporting documentation, and the situation will typically be reviewed by other clinicians at the health plan. The grievance procedure depends on the severity of the accusation and the number of grievances previously filed against you. But the emphasis is on improving quality of care and member service, not punishment, so most insurance plans will work with providers toward this end, whenever possible.

How should I handle a client in an emergency?

Since emergency phone sessions are not typically covered by insurance plans (unless pre-approved), you may want to schedule a session as soon as possible. But therapists should not hesitate to tell callers to dial 911 or go directly to the emergency room if they believe the client is experiencing a life-threatening emergency. Most plans cover emergency services. In fact, some states have laws that forbid plans from denying payment for emergency services, even if the situation was later discovered not to be an emergency -- if any prudent layperson would have considered it to be an emergency. Outgoing messages on your office answering machine should also direct clients to call 911 or go to the emergency room in an emergency.

Will the insurance plan cover Eye Movement Desensitization Reprocessing (EMDR) or hypnosis?

This varies by insurance company. Plans tend to be a bit traditional. However, according to a CIGNA Behavioral Health spokeswoman, in 2005 about 1,500 of CIGNA's 60,000 network members were certified to bill for EMDR, and in these cases were allowed to bill for two-hour sessions[28]. One client I knew could not find an EMDR therapist on her health plan, and convinced her case manager to sign a Single-Case Agreement with an EMDR-trained therapist in her area. Some companies, like Managed Health Network, will pay for EMDR, but not as a "stand-alone" treatment[29]. Others won't reimburse for EMDR at all. Hypnosis is often covered, but usually only as one part of a treatment plan.

Tip: When you write anything in a client's records, always be mindful that some insurance representative or another treating health professional may someday review it. Records should be in ink or typed, legible, dated, and in chronological order, giving evidence to your thought processes behind diagnoses, referrals, and treatment plan. This is not just for insurance clients -- this is just good sense for all your cases, to protect you in case of a lawsuit or ethical charge filed against you. Document any history of violence, and use of cigarettes, alcohol, and drugs (illicit, prescription, and over-the-counter), or other risk factors.

11
Getting Paid
Submitting Claims and Giving Invoices

ଧ୍ଧ ଔ

You have been working with Jack for a month now, and you decide to submit your bills for your sessions to CureQuick.

Now I know you are in this line of work because you care so much about humankind. But let's face it, we've all got expenses to pay! So understanding the insurance billing and payment process is especially important. This knowledge is essential even if you never join a provider network, as in all likelihood you will be providing some type of invoice to many clients to submit to their insurance plan.

Let's review the billing differences for in-network and out-of-network providers:

As a Participating Provider

- You should put your full fee on the claim form, not your contracted rate. An adjustment will be made by the insurance plan before you are paid.

- You have probably agreed in your contract to take care of billing CureQuick on Jack's behalf. Jack pays only the co-payment or co-insurance, and any deductible, if applicable.

- You have agreed to accept CureQuick's rate as reimbursement in full for your services. You cannot "balance-bill," which means you cannot charge Jack for the difference between your full fee and the discounted amount CureQuick pays you.

If You Were an Out-of-Network Provider

- You can charge Jack your full fee for the session. There is no fee discount, unless you are offering the client a sliding scale fee.

- You may balance-bill (charge Jack for the difference between the amount CureQuick pays you and your full fee). In fact, it may be considered fraud not to balance-bill.

- You may have Jack pay your full fee and give him an invoice to submit to his insurance plan, or you may collect only the co-payment/co-insurance and any deductible (if applicable) and bill the insurance plan for the balance (see sample invoice, Page 147).

Does being an out-of network provider sound good right now? Of course. But remember that only network providers receive referrals from the insurance plan, and Jack would not have come to you without this referral.

The Revised CMS-1500 Claim Form (formerly the HCFA-1500)

While a few insurance plans and many EAPs require that you use their own claim form, the CMS-1500 is the standard claim form accepted by most plans. Distributed by the Center for Medicare and Medicaid Services, this form is often still called the HCFA-1500, its former name when the CMS was the Health Care Financing Administration. This form can be used by solo practitioners, groups, and facilities billing for outpatient services (if you are a facility billing for inpatient services or an intensive outpatient program, you may need to use a UB-92 form instead).

WARNING!! A revised version of the CMS-1500 is now required by most plans! Released in July of 2006, this revision (version 08/05) was made primarily to accommodate the new National Provider Identifier (NPI) that some providers were required to obtain as part of recent HIPAA laws (see Chapter 7). **You can tell you have the revised form if you see the number "1500" in a circle in the top left corner, and "08/05" at the bottom left.** At the time of this printing, most health plans stated they were requiring (or would soon be requiring) this new version. However, it is recommended that you contact the health plans you work with prior to submitting a claim on the revised form to ensure they are prepared to accept it (for ideas where to get these forms, see Resources, Page 133).

A sample of the revised form appears on the next page. Following that is a chart that gives line-by-line instructions and tips for filling out the form. A few notes:

- **Handwritten or copied?** The example on the next page shows a computer-printed claim. But can you handwrite these forms or copy them? For fastest processing, many health plans recommend (and some may soon insist) that your claims be:
  1. Submitted on the original red CMS-1500 forms,
  2. Typed or computer-printed, using black ink, with block capital letters, and
  3. Free of crossed-out or typed-over mistakes.

  Why? According to Brad Lotterman of United Behavioral Health, "UBH receives more than 2,000 illegible handwritten claims a day.[30]" In addition, most plans have computer scanners that can only read typed characters on original red forms. This means photocopied and/or handwritten claims will require hand-processing, thus delaying your payment. And it won't help if you print the forms using red ink from your printer! Your red ink isn't the same as the one on the forms, so it can't be optically scanned by the insurance plan's computer.

- **Submit via mail, fax, or electronically?** This is up to you and the insurance plan, but electronic billing leads to fastest payment (see Chapter 14 for more on electronic billing).

The (Revised) CMS-1500, formerly the HCFA-1500

HEALTH INSURANCE CLAIM FORM
APPROVED BY NATIONAL UNIFORM CLAIM COMMITTEE 08/05

CUREQUICK INSURANCE INC.
P.O. BOX 4456
PAPER TRAIL, MN 55344

CARRIER

☐☐ PICA | PICA ☐☐

1. MEDICARE (Medicare #)	MEDICAID (Medicaid #)	TRICARE CHAMPUS (Sponsor's SSN)	CHAMPVA (Member ID#)	GROUP HEALTH PLAN (SSN or ID) [X]	FECA BLK LUNG (SSN)	OTHER (ID)	1a. INSURED'S I.D. NUMBER (For Program in item 1)

1a. INSURED'S I.D. NUMBER: **PRU34567-00**

2. PATIENT'S NAME (Last Name, First Name, Middle Initial): **KLUTZ, JACK**

3. PATIENT'S BIRTH DATE MM | DD | YY: **02 | 01 | 1961** SEX M [X] F ☐

4. INSURED'S NAME (Last Name, First Name, Middle Initial): **KLUTZ, JACK**

5. PATIENT'S ADDRESS (No., Street): **123 WATER STREET**

6. PATIENT RELATIONSHIP TO INSURED: Self [X] Spouse ☐ Child ☐ Other ☐

7. INSURED'S ADDRESS (No., Street): **123 WATER STREET**

CITY: **HILLTOWN** STATE: **CA**

8. PATIENT STATUS: Single ☐ Married [X] Other ☐

CITY: **HILLTOWN** STATE: **CA**

ZIP CODE: **95128** TELEPHONE (Include Area Code): **(408) 5551234**

Employed [X] Full-Time Student ☐ Part-Time Student ☐

ZIP CODE: **95128** TELEPHONE (Include Area Code): **(408) 5551234**

9. OTHER INSURED'S NAME (Last Name, First Name, Middle Initial):

10. IS PATIENT'S CONDITION RELATED TO:

11. INSURED'S POLICY GROUP OR FECA NUMBER: **H00123**

a. OTHER INSURED'S POLICY OR GROUP NUMBER:

a. EMPLOYMENT? (Current or Previous) YES ☐ NO [X]

a. INSURED'S DATE OF BIRTH MM | DD | YY: **02 | 01 | 1961** SEX M [X] F ☐

b. OTHER INSURED'S DATE OF BIRTH MM | DD | YY SEX M ☐ F ☐

b. AUTO ACCIDENT? PLACE (State) YES ☐ NO [X]

b. EMPLOYER'S NAME OR SCHOOL NAME: **PAILS-R-US**

c. EMPLOYER'S NAME OR SCHOOL NAME:

c. OTHER ACCIDENT? YES ☐ NO [X]

c. INSURANCE PLAN NAME OR PROGRAM NAME: **WONDERFUL OPTIMA HMO**

d. INSURANCE PLAN NAME OR PROGRAM NAME:

10d. RESERVED FOR LOCAL USE

d. IS THERE ANOTHER HEALTH BENEFIT PLAN? YES ☐ NO [X] If yes, return to and complete item 9 a-d.

READ BACK OF FORM BEFORE COMPLETING & SIGNING THIS FORM.

12. PATIENT'S OR AUTHORIZED PERSON'S SIGNATURE I authorize the release of any medical or other information necessary to process this claim. I also request payment of government benefits either to myself or to the party who accepts assignment below.

SIGNED **SIGNATURE ON FILE** DATE **03 24 2008**

13. INSURED'S OR AUTHORIZED PERSON'S SIGNATURE I authorize payment of medical benefits to the undersigned physician or supplier for services described below.

SIGNED **SIGNATURE ON FILE**

14. DATE OF CURRENT: ILLNESS (First symptom) OR INJURY (Accident) OR PREGNANCY (LMP) MM | DD | YY: **01 | 14 | 2008**

15. IF PATIENT HAS HAD SAME OR SIMILAR ILLNESS, GIVE FIRST DATE MM | DD | YY

16. DATES PATIENT UNABLE TO WORK IN CURRENT OCCUPATION FROM MM DD YY TO MM DD YY

17. NAME OF REFERRING PROVIDER OR OTHER SOURCE

17a.
17b. NPI

18. HOSPITALIZATION DATES RELATED TO CURRENT SERVICES FROM MM DD YY TO MM DD YY

19. RESERVED FOR LOCAL USE

20. OUTSIDE LAB? YES ☐ NO [X] $ CHARGES

21. DIAGNOSIS OR NATURE OF ILLNESS OR INJURY. (Relate Items 1,2,3 or 4 to Item 24E by Line)

1. **309 81** 3. |_____
2. **305 20** 4. |_____

22. MEDICAID RESUBMISSION CODE | ORIGINAL REF. NO.

23. PRIOR AUTHORIZATION NUMBER: **1005678**

24. A. DATE(S) OF SERVICE From MM DD YY	To MM DD YY	B. PLACE OF SERVICE	C. EMG	D. PROCEDURES, SERVICES, OR SUPPLIES (Explain Unusual Circumstances) CPT/HCPCS	MODIFIER	E. DIAGNOSIS POINTER	F. $ CHARGES	G. DAYS OR UNITS	H. EPSDT Family Plan	I. ID. QUAL.	J. RENDERING PROVIDER ID. #
1	02 01 08	02 01 08	11		90801		1	110 00	1		0B / NPI	MFC27210 / 1386652212
2	02 08 08	02 08 08	11		90806		1	100 00	1		0B / NPI	MFC27210 / 1386652212
3	02 15 08	02 15 08	11		90847		1 2	100 00	1		0B / NPI	MFC27210 / 1386652212
4	02 22 08	02 22 08	11		90806		1 2	100 00	1		0B / NPI	MFC27210 / 1386652212
5											NPI	
6											NPI	

25. FEDERAL TAX I.D. NUMBER: **156421844** SSN ☐ EIN [X]

26. PATIENT'S ACCOUNT NO.

27. ACCEPT ASSIGNMENT? (For govt. claims, see back) [X] YES ☐ NO

28. TOTAL CHARGE $ **410 00**

29. AMOUNT PAID $

30. BALANCE DUE $ **410 00**

31. SIGNATURE OF PHYSICIAN OR SUPPLIER INCLUDING DEGREES OR CREDENTIALS (I certify that the statements on the reverse apply to this bill and are made a part thereof.)
BARBARA C. GRISWOLD, M.S., MFT
Barbara C. Griswold LMFT SIGNED **03 24 2008** DATE

32. SERVICE FACILITY LOCATION INFORMATION
OFFICE
4100 MOORPARK AVENUE #116
SAN JOSE CA 95117
a. 1386652212 b. 0BMFC27210

33. BILLING PROVIDER INFO & PH. # **(408) 9850846**
BARBARA C GRISWOLD, M S, LMFT
4100 MOORPARK AVENUE, SUITE 116
SAN JOSE CA 95117
a. 1386652212 b. 0BMFC27210

NUCC Instruction Manual available at: www.nucc.org

APPROVED OMB 0938-0999 FORM CMS-1500 (08/05)

Box	How to Compete the CMS-1500 Claim Form
Top of Form	Type or neatly print the insurance company's name and the claims address on the upper right-hand corner of the form.
1	Identify the type of health plan with an "X". Mark only one box. This will usually be "Group Health Plan" if the client is using a plan sponsored by an employer, club, or professional association.
1a	Enter the ID number from the client's ID card. This is the insurance plan's ID number of the person who holds the policy. Don't forget the letter prefix, if any. While Social Security Numbers used to be the ID, in response to recent laws and identity theft concerns, many insurance plans have assigned different ID numbers. Use the policyholder's Social Security Number if you don't have an ID number.
2	The <u>client's</u> full name. Last name first, then a comma, then first name. No nicknames or titles. <u>Do not write "SAME" in this or any other field</u>, even if the information is the same as in Item 4; <u>the electronic scanner won't understand this</u>. With couples or families, pick an identified client (s/he must have a diagnosis).
3	Client's birth date in 8-digit MM/DD/CCYY format. Put an "X" in box of gender.
4	The <u>insured's</u> name goes here. The insured (or subscriber) is the primary holder of the insurance – the person whose insurance the client is using. In employer-sponsored plans, this would be the employee. Last name first, then a comma, then first name. No nicknames or titles. Don't write "SAME," even if the information is the same as in Item 2.
5	<u>Client's</u> permanent mailing address (use two-letter state abbreviation) and phone number. Do not use punctuation in the address (except hyphen if entering 9-digit ZIP code). Do not use a hyphen/space to separate the last 7 digits of the phone number. Do not write "SAME," even if the information is the same as Item 7.
6	How is the client related to the insured? Put an "X" in the appropriate box. "Spouse" includes qualified partners, as defined by the plan.
7	<u>Insured's</u> permanent mailing address (use two-letter state abbreviation) and phone number. Do not use punctuation in the address (except hyphen if entering 9-digit ZIP code). Do not use a hyphen/space to separate the last 7 digits of phone number. Do not write "SAME," even if the information is the same as Item 5.
8	Put an "X" to indicate client's marital and employment status. In second row, leave boxes blank if none apply (i.e. if client is unemployed and not a student).
9 a-d	Leave blank unless the client is covered by more than one insurance plan, or you are seeing a couple or family and you (or they) intend to eventually bill each client's plans for the session. For more about "double coverage," such as how to figure out which plan is primary, see Page ___. In this box, enter the information about the secondary plan. Last name of secondary policy holder first, then a comma, then first name. Answer a-d as they apply to the person in Question 9. Do not use a hyphen/space within the policy or group number. Enter the 8-digit date of birth (MM/DD/CCYY) of the person named in Question 9, and mark the gender with an "X." Identify the other employer's name, and the secondary plan.
10 a-c	Are symptoms related to a condition or injury that occurred on the job, or as a result of an auto accident or other accident? If "yes," there may be other applicable coverage that would be primary, such as automobile liability insurance.
10 d	Leave blank, unless instructed otherwise by the insurance plan.
11	Fill in the client's group number from the insurance card. Do not use hyphens/spaces within the policy or group number.

11 a-c	Enter the 8-digit date of birth (DD/MM/CCYY) of insured person named in Box 4. Enter gender, employer, and insurance plan name. This helps identify the name of the plan and which type of plan the client is using (e.g. HMO, POS, EPO, PPO, EAP)
11 d	Check "yes" if the client is covered by more than one insurance plan or if you are seeing a couple or family and you (or your clients) have the intent to bill both plans (see instructions for Box 9, and "Double Coverage" on Page 106). If your response here is "yes," also complete Box 9 and 9a-d. Otherwise, check "no."
12	Have the client sign here and date to authorize the release of information to the insurance plan to process this claim, and keep a copy in the client record. Once you have the signature in your file, you may write "Signature on File" on future claims. Some therapists incorporate the wording from Box 12 into their treatment agreement or a separate release form and have the client sign and date that instead (see sample agreement, Page 145). If you do this, you may write "Signature On File" in this box on all claims, even the initial one. Do not put any text in this box other than "Signature on File" or the client's signature. Parents/guardians should sign if the client is a minor.
13	<u>Leave this box blank if you want the plan to reimburse the client directly.</u> If you want the insurance plan to pay you, have the client sign this box. Again, some therapists incorporate the wording from Box 12 into their treatment agreement or a separate release form and have the client sign and date that instead (see sample agreement, Page 145). If you do this, you may write "Signature On File" in this box on all claims, even the initial one. Do not put any text in this box other than "Signature on File," or the client's signature. Parents/guardians should sign if the client is a minor.
14	Fill in estimated 6- or 8-digit date the symptoms began for current condition.
15	If client has had this or a similar condition before, estimate the 6-digit or 8-digit date when the client had a previous related condition. This is not required by most plans.
16	Leave blank, unless the client is (or was recently) unable to work. Give the 6-digit or 8-digit start and end dates of the time span the client is/was unable to work. If still unable to work, leave the end time blank.
17	You may leave blank, unless a doctor's referral is required for treatment.
17a	Leave blank, unless a doctor's referral is required for treatment. If the referring physician has a National Provider Identifier, leave this box blank, and enter the NPI in Box 17b. If the doctor has no NPI, then fill in an alternate ID number here (see instructions for Box 24 I and J for acceptable ID numbers and their prefixes). Put the prefix in the first box to the right of the "17a," then the ID number in the box to the right of this box.
17b	Leave blank, unless a doctor's referral is required for treatment. Record the referring physician's National Provider Identifier. If s/he has no NPI, see instructions for Box 17a.
18	Leave blank, unless the client had a recent related hospitalization. Give the 6- or 8-digit admission and discharge dates. If still in the hospital, leave discharge date blank.
19-20	You may leave blank, unless otherwise instructed by insurer.
21	Fill in the diagnosis or diagnoses, listing the primary first. List up to four diagnoses, <u>which typically must come from the ICD,</u> the American Medical Association's *International Classification of Diseases*[31] (see Resources, Page 133). <u>A claim may be rejected if you do not use the full number of possible digits</u> for the diagnosis (e.g. if you write 296.3 instead of 296.33). <u>Most diagnoses need 5 digits, but some are only 3 or 4.</u> Use only codes, not descriptions. Do not defer the diagnosis: Choose one(s) you believe fits best. V-codes alone are not usually reimbursed. As in the example on Page 61, if you add a diagnosis at any point in the billing period, include both (or all) here.

22	You may leave blank, unless dealing with Medicaid.
23	Write the authorization number here, if applicable. Do not enter spaces or hyphens within the number. If the session dates fall on more than one authorization (e.g., you've used the last three sessions of one authorization and the first of another), write both authorization numbers here. Even if you have an authorization, this box is not required by all plans.
24 A	Below Box 24A, you will see lines numbered 1 through 6. These are divided, each with a gray shaded portion on top, and white portion underneath. Ignore the shaded portion, and list session dates in the lower white portion of each line of this column (the "Dates of Service or "DOS" in MM/DD/YY format), listing <u>one date of service per line</u>.
24 B	Enter the two-digit code from the Place-Of-Service Code list to indicate where the session took place. <u>Do not write "O," "OV" or "Office."</u> Write "11" if you saw the client in an office or clinic. Do not use quotation marks or write "SAME" to indicate duplicate information. Other codes include 12 (home), 51 (inpatient psychiatric facility), 22 (psychiatric facility, partial hospitalization), 53 (community mental health center), 53 (freestanding psychiatric facility), and 99 (other unlisted facility). See Resources on Page 133 for the Web site where you can download the entire code list.
24 C	You may leave blank, unless otherwise directed.
24 D	Enter the CPT (Current Procedural Terminology) code for your service[32]. These codes from the American Medical Association identify the type of service provided. You may have only been given an authorization to provide certain types of service, or CPT codes. But remember: It is fraud to alter the code in order to be reimbursed, or be reimbursed at a higher rate. Leave the column under "Modifier" blank, unless instructed otherwise. Do not use quotation marks to indicate duplicate information. **<u>CPT codes frequently used by therapists in an office setting</u>:** **90801**: Psychiatric diagnostic examination *(Many plans cover only one of these)* **90806**: Individual psychotherapy, approximately 45 to 50 minutes face-to-face with the patient **90846**: Family psychotherapy (without patient present) **90847**: Family psychotherapy (conjoint psychotherapy with patient present) **90812**: Individual psychotherapy, interactive, using play equipment or other mechanisms of nonverbal communication in an office or outpatient facility, approximately 45 to 50 minutes face-to-face with the patient **90849**: Multiple-family group psychotherapy **90853**: Group psychotherapy (other than of a multiple-family group) **90857**: Interactive group psychotherapy To get the complete list of CPT codes, see "Resources," Page 133. *CPT codes © American Medical Association. All rights reserved.*
24 E	For each date of service, note which diagnoses from Box 21 that you treated in that session (e.g., if you focused on the first diagnosis you listed, write "1" for that date of service). If you focused on more than one diagnosis, you may enter up to 4 numbers, without commas between them (e.g., "12" or "134"). As in the example on Page 61, if you add a diagnosis during the billing period, it may be reflected by an additional number in this column. Don't use quotation marks to indicate duplicate information.

24 F	Write your normal fee (not the contracted rate) for the listed service. The plan will automatically adjust it if you have agreed to a fee discount. Do not use commas, periods, or dollar signs. Enter 00 in the cents area if a whole number. Don't use quotation marks to indicate duplicate information.
24 G	Indicate sessions or number of units of service billed on that line, usually one. Don't use quotation marks to indicate duplicate information.
24 H	You may leave blank, unless otherwise indicated by the plan.
24 I and J	In Column J you will give the ID of the treating provider for each date of service. Column I tells which type of ID number you will be giving in Column J. Note: In the sample claim o61, I show examples of both how to list your NPI and your non-NPI (legacy number) in this box. <u>You only need one or the other</u>. Remember if you bill electronically (via the Internet), you must use a NPI. **If you have a National Provider Identifier,** skip Column I and fill in your NPI in the white area of Column J <u>for each date of service</u> (see sample claim on Page 61). **If you don't have a NPI,** you'll need to choose another type of ID number (often called a "legacy number") from the approved list that follows. Each is shown with a 2-digit prefix, or "qualifier." 0B State license number G2 Provider Commercial Number 1B Blue Shield Provider Number LU Location Numbers 1C Medicare Provider Number N5 Provider Plan Network ID Number ID Medicaid Provider Number SY Social Security number 1G Provider UPIN Number X5 State Industrial Accident Provider Number IH CHAMPUS ID Number ZZ Provider Taxonomy E1 Employer's Identification Number If you don't have an NPI, for each session fill in Column I (above the letters "NPI") with the qualifier code that identifies the ID number you are using in Column J. <u>Use the shaded portion of these boxes for each line.</u> In Column J, enter the non-NPI number in the shaded area (see example to the right, and sample claim on Page 61). <table><tr><td>I ID Qual.</td><td>J. Rendering Provider ID</td></tr><tr><td>0B</td><td>MFC27210</td></tr><tr><td>NPI</td><td></td></tr></table> *Example: State License Number*
25	Claims must have a tax ID number for tax purposes, even if you use a NPI or legacy number elsewhere on the form. Do not enter hyphens. Indicate if this is your Social Security Number (SSN) or Employer Identification Number (EIN). If you prefer not to use your Social Security Number (to avoid identity theft), you may consider getting an EIN. This number is simple to get and free to obtain (see Resources on Page 133 for where to apply). However, if you have been using your SSN on claims, you will need to submit an IRS W-9 form to each health plan, alerting them of your new EIN tax identification number. One colleague I spoke with had claims denied despite the fact that he had submitted all the proper paperwork to the health plans.
26	You may skip. If you assign clients an account number, you may record it here.
27	Enter an "X" in the "Yes" box if you are asking that payment be made to you; enter an "X" in the "No" box if payment should be made to the client. If you do not mark one of these, your claim may be rejected.
28	Add the total of all individual line charges on the page. Do not use commas, periods, or dollar signs. Enter 00 in the cents area if the amount is a whole number.

29-30	I do not recommend you write in this box. While you may be tempted to write what clients have paid you, this is unnecessary, <u>and sometimes causes claim problems.</u> The insurance company will calculate what it owes without this information.
31	Print or type your name and sign here, <u>including degree and/or license</u>, and date. While interns or associates typically are not reimbursed by insurance, some plans do allow this. If you have the health plan's approval, the intern/associate <u>and</u> supervisor should both sign, and titles such as "treating therapist" and "supervising therapist" should be used to clearly indicate roles. You may not give the appearance that the supervisor performed the therapy – this would be fraud. Enter either the 6-digit date, 8-digit date, or alphanumeric date (e.g., February 24, 2008) when the form was signed.
32 and 32 a-b	Enter the name and address of the location where the services were rendered. Do not use commas, periods, or other punctuation in the address. If the service location is your office, use your NPI number in 32a (if you have one) and skip 32b. Remember if you bill electronically (via the Internet), you must use a NPI. If the service site is an agency that has a NPI, use their NPI in 32a, and skip 32b. If you or the facility do not have a NPI, leave 32a blank, and in Box 32b give one of the "legacy" ID types from the following list. The number should be preceded by the 2-digit "qualifier" code prefix that identifies the type of non-NPI ID number you are using: 0B State license number G2 Provider Commercial Number 1A Blue Cross Provider Number LU Location Number 1B Blue Shield Provider Number N5 Provider Plan Network ID Number 1C Medicare Provider Number TJ Federal Taxpayer's Identification Number ID Medicaid Provider Number X4 Clinical Lab. Improvement Amendment No. 1G Provider UPIN Number X5 State Industrial Accident Provider Number IH CHAMPUS ID Number ZZ Provider Taxonomy <u>You will note this list differs from the one in Box 24 Column I.</u> Don't use a space, hyphen, or other separator between the prefix and number. The prefix should be followed by the non-NPI number in the shaded area. Note: In the sample claim on Page 61, I show examples of both how to list your NPI and your non-NPI (legacy number) in this box. <u>You only need one or the other.</u>
33 and 33 a-b	Print your name, or the group or facility (if applicable) who is doing the billing. Include your degree, license, billing address, and phone number. Your billing address is not always the same as the location where you provided the services. Enter your phone number in upper right portion of the box; do not use a hyphen or space as a separator within the phone number. Do not use commas, periods, or other punctuation in address, except hyphens if you use a 9-digit ZIP code. **If you (or your facility) have a National Provider Identifier,** write it in Box 33a, and skip 33b. Remember if you bill electronically (via the Internet), you must use a NPI. **If you don't have a NPI,** skip 33a, and in 33b give a "legacy" ID from the list below. The number should be preceded by the 2-digit qualifier code that identifies the ID: 0B State license number BQ Health Maintenance Organization Code No. 1A Blue Cross Provider Number FH Clinic Number 1B Blue Shield Provider Number G2 Provider Commercial Number 1C Medicare Provider Number G5 Provider Site Number ID Medicaid Provider Number LU Location Number 1G Provider UPIN Number U3 Unique Supplier Identification Number IH CHAMPUS ID Number X5 State Industrial Accident Provider Number IJ Facility ID Number ZZ Provider Taxonomy B3 Preferred Provider Organization Number *(continued)*

33 and 33 a-b (cont.)	*(continued)* You will notice this list differs somewhat from the lists in Box 24 Column I and the one in Box 32b. The prefix should be followed by the non-NPI number in 33b. Don't use a hyphen or separator between the prefix and the legacy number. Note: In the sample claim on Page 61, I show examples of both how to list your NPI and your non-NPI (legacy number) in this box. You only need one or the other. Remember if you bill electronically (via the Internet), you must use a NPI. If your client was seen at a facility or group, and they are billing for the service, use their NPI or ID number, not yours.

This chart adapted from the National Uniform Claim Committee's 1500 Claim Form Instruction Manual[33].

A Few General Claims Tips

- **Record the date you submitted the claim** in a ledger, computer, or the client's chart (see sample Service Record on Page 149).

- **Keep a copy of all claims you submit.**

- **Be sure you sign all claims.**

- **Fill out forms slowly, neatly, and carefully.** Proofread them before sending them. A simple oversight or illegible entry could delay payment by weeks – or longer.

- **Leaving blanks is OK.** This form is used by many types of health care providers, so some questions will not apply to psychotherapists. Don't write "not applicable" or "n/a."

- **In certain situations, it is a good idea to submit a completed Coordination of Benefits (COB) form** with the first claim. This form was developed for situations when the client is covered by more than one health plan, or to help the client's plan find out if there is another coverage plan that might be primary or secondary. This coordination prevents a provider from collecting more than their full fee from two insurance plans. For example, if Jack is employed, but you are submitting his claim to Jill's insurance plan, her plan might wonder why Jack's insurance plan isn't footing the bill. Without this form, CureQuick may pend (delay processing of) the claim until they receive it. The COB form is usually available from the insurance plan (you can download it from their Web site, or have them fax it to you). For more on "double coverage," see Page 106.

Questions and Answers

Do all plans accept CMS-1500s?

No, but most do. Some plans, particularly employee assistance programs, may require that their own billing forms be used instead.

Do I have to fill out a new form every time I bill?

No. One therapist I know fills out the form after the first session, leaving the session dates, CPT codes, signature, date, and session-specific information blank. Then she uses this as her original. Each time she bills, she simply makes a copy, fills in the new information, signs, and submits it.

However, as was previously mentioned, insurance plans prefer bills to be on original red CMS-1500 claim forms, and these are usually paid more rapidly, since they are may be computer-scanned.

Will insurance cover phone sessions, or can I bill the client directly?

At one time or another, we have all probably provided therapy on the phone, such as when a client was in an after-hours crisis, or when she was unable to come to your office due to transportation problems, illness, or child-care difficulties. However, most insurance companies don't cover telephone sessions. U.S. Behavioral Health Plan California states that its plan will reimburse for telephone counseling in situations "when clinically necessary and appropriate," but that all phone sessions must be pre-approved[34]. If you do bill for a telephone session, you would need to use a CPT code for this (ex. 99371, 99372, 99373), as it would be fraud if you gave the appearance that you met face-to-face with the client.

If the plan does not cover phone calls, some plans will allow you to bill the client for the phone call only when he has as he signed an agreement in advance to pay for phone sessions. Some contracts may limit your charge to your contracted rate, if you have a contract with his insurance plan. When I asked one case manager why her company did not pay for extended crisis-management calls, she said they felt that the fee they paid for sessions included any telephone calls made to (or on behalf of) the client outside the session. "You will have some clients that need a lot of phone time, some that require little or none," she explained. "The fee we pay is an average of both."

Will insurers pay for e-mail sessions?

While traditionally insurance companies have not paid for online sessions, this may be changing. *Open Minds* newsletter quotes *The Wall Street Journal:* "Participating firms, therapists, and payers are establishing protocols for remote counseling through instant messaging (IM) and e-mail ... Some employee assistance programs offer electronic or on-line support as part of a wellness or disease management program[35]." The *Open Minds* article goes on to say that insurance plans like CIGNA Behavioral Health are covering at least one approved drug and alcohol online counseling program, and Managed Health Network has a smoking-cessation program that includes an online support component.

What about no-shows or late-cancelled sessions? Can I bill insurance or the client?

Most insurance companies will not cover missed sessions. One exception may be if the managed care company contacted you to set up an urgent or emergency appointment -- the plan will sometimes reimburse you if that client does not show up. Contact the insurance plan or check your contract for their policy on missed sessions. As for EAPs, some pay for missed sessions, some don't. The member may lose one EAP session for each no-show. One EAP plan I work with pays

$25 for the first missed session only. If you do bill for a missed session, clearly indicate that it was a missed or late-cancelled session on the claim form. <u>Don't make it look like a face-to-face therapy session took place -- this is insurance fraud.</u>

As to whether or not you can charge the client for the missed session, contracts vary on this issue. You may not be able to charge your client for these sessions, or you may only be able to charge your discounted contracted rate. Many insurance companies allow you to bill the client for these sessions only if the client has agreed in advance (and in writing) to pay for missed sessions. This can be easily accomplished by having a line devoted to this in your treatment agreement (see sample treatment agreement, Page 145).

How often do I need to bill insurance?

I recommend you at least bill monthly. All therapists develop their own system. It's wise to submit your first claim shortly after treatment has begun, to find out early if there are any problems. Obviously, the more often you bill, the more frequently those payment checks roll in! Going too long between billings can also bring big headaches. I have seen cases where therapists allowed large balances to accumulate, only to face trouble when the insurance company didn't pay. Also, <u>many insurance plans have time limitations on claims -- some will not pay if they receive the bill more than 60 or 90 days after the date of service.</u> Read your contract.

My personal routine is to bill monthly. At the beginning of February, for example, I prepare and send out claims for all insurance clients I saw in January, making a note in the client's chart of the date I sent the claim (see sample Service Record on Page 149). I also check to see if I have been paid for all previously submitted claims.

How long should I wait before I call the insurance plan if I haven't been paid?

Blue Cross suggests waiting 30 working days for PPO plans and 45 working days for HMO plans. I'd recommend that you call if you haven't received a response from any plan within six weeks if you submitted by mail, four weeks if you submitted online or electronically. Many plans offer the option of tracking claim status online. If they say they didn't receive it, they may ask you to resubmit the claim. You may consider asking them if you can fax it to expedite processing. Don't forget to document your call, who you spoke to, and what you were told. If you resubmit it via mail, attach a Post-It Note that says "second submission," so that if it is after the claim submission deadline the plan will still accept it.

Will the insurance plan reimburse me for the time I spend filling out paperwork?

Dream on. This is VERY rare. If you do try to bill for paperwork time, use the CPT code for this.

What if my client is covered by two insurance plans?

Ah, now things get interesting. See "Double Coverage" in Chapter 17.

What if I make a mistake on a bill I've already sent in?

It depends on the mistake. Call and ask how the insurance plan would like you to handle it. You may be asked to submit a corrected claim (a duplicate of the original claim you sent — without the mistake). Attach a note (Post-It Notes are fine) stating that it is a corrected claim, or it may be rejected as a "duplicate claim."

My claim was denied because I was late submitting it. Can I bill the client?

If you are a network provider, there is a good chance the provider contract you signed won't allow this. Read the contract. If you are an out-of-network provider, you may bill the client.

If my client pays me in full, what kind of bill do I give him so he can be reimbursed?

I'm assuming you are an out-of-network provider, since insurance plans usually require their network providers to bill the plan on the client's behalf.

You can either 1) give him a completed CMS-1500 form (leaving Box 13 blank and checking "No" in Box 27) or 2) give him your own personalized billing invoice/statement/superbill (a sample can be found on Page 147). On your invoice, be sure to include all the necessary information needed for reimbursement, including diagnosis, CPT codes, Place-of-Service codes, your NPI (if you have one) and your provider ID number (i.e. Social Security Number or Employer Identification Number). In other words, put on your invoice all the important information from the bottom half of the CMS-1500 form. When submitting an invoice, your client may need to attach it to a completed billing form from his insurance company. If the plan accepts the CMS-1500 form, your client could attach your invoice to a CMS-1500 form, and s/he would need to complete Boxes 1-13 of the CMS form.

How do I bill for a one-and-a-half or two hour session? Should I just bill insurance for one hour, since that is all the plan will pay, and bill the client for the rest?

Many insurance plans will only cover one hour of outpatient therapy per day (some only allow one hour per week). If the plan allows a longer session, typically this would require pre-approval from the plan for the special circumstances. An insurance representative I queried said it could be considered fraud to report a one-hour session when you actually provided a longer one. She advised that the claim (or invoice) should reflect the actual session length provided; the plan will simply pay their maximum (which may be the amount for a one-hour session). This may not be how all plans want you to handle this situation. As always, I recommend that you contact the plan for coding advice.

You may be able to find the CPT code that fits your actual session length. If the code you are using does not specify session length, if you provided a two-hour session you might indicate "2" in the "Days or Units" column (24G on the CMS-1500). Another option is to attach the modifier -22 to the CPT code of the service provided (under the word "Modifier" in Box 24D), to indicate the session was longer than the usual time period for that service. But if you don't contact the plan first, you run the risk of claim rejection when you use an unusual or unauthorized CPT code.

Can I charge the client interest on overdue co-payments or deductibles?

Many contracts forbid this. Some allow this if the client has agreed in advance (and in writing) to this policy. Read your contract or provider handbook, or contact the insurance company.

Can I bill for sessions from two separate months, or two separate years (such as December of one year and January of the next) on one claim form?

It's no problem to bill for more than one month on one bill. However, some insurance companies prefer that you divide charges from two separate calendar (or coverage) years into separate claims (e.g., one for December charges, one for January) instead of submitting a "split-year" claim.

Can I submit a claim for EAP and non-EAP sessions on the same form?

As was mentioned in Chapter 3, many EAPs require their own claim form, so you may not be able to use the same form for both EAP and routine mental health sessions. Also, EAP claims may need to be sent to a different claims address than regular mental health claims, even if being processed by the same insurance plan. But even if the insurance plan allows both types of sessions to be billed on CMS-1500 forms, it is wise to separate EAP and non-EAP claims on different forms. They may need to be processed separately, and combining them may delay payment. Remember that some plans even have their own CPT codes for EAP sessions.

12

The Check Arrives — or Doesn't
The Explanation of Benefits and Claim Denials

ଉ ଓ

Weeks after submitting your claim for Jack's sessions, you practically kiss the mail carrier when you see his bag holds an envelope from CureQuick. Before you dance on your desk to celebrate your reward for fine therapy, you take a moment to look more closely at the paperwork you've received.

Inside the envelope you find an Explanation of Benefits (EOB) like the sample below. An EOB is a statement that outlines how the claim was processed, shows any deductions made for co-payments, co-insurance, or deductibles, and shows the final net payment (if any) to you or the client. If you requested reimbursement, and all has gone well, a check is attached. A copy of the EOB is also sent to the policy holder; this may not be the client.

CureQuick Behavioral Health
P.O. Box 4455
Paper Trail, MN 55344
800-555-1234

EXPLANATION OF BENEFITS

ISSUE DATE March 24, 2008	CHECK NUMBER 0002795220

Control Number   0010388563
Provider Tax ID   156421844
CUREQUICK VENDOR ID: 67750

BARBARA GRISWOLD, LMFT
4100 MOORPARK AVE. #116
SAN JOSE, CA   95117

Patient Name: KLUTZ, JACK   ID Number: PRU34567-00 Acct. Nbr: 90 Group: HOO123
Claim ID: 05222451522   Claim Received: 02/29/08   **CUREQUICK BH AGREEMENT**

Service Date	Procedure Code	Billed Amount	Allowed Amount	Not Allowed	Deductible	Co-insurance/ Co-payment	Claims Payment
02/01/08	90801	110.00	75.00	35.00 / 01		15.00	60.00
02/08/06	90806	100.00	67.00	33.00 / 01		13.40	53.60
02/15/06	90847	100.00	75.00	25.00 / 01		15.00	60.00
02/22/06	90806	100.00	67.00	33.00 / 01		13.40	53.60
TOTALS:		**410.00**	**284.00**	**126.00**		**56.80**	**227.20**

01 – This is the amount in excess of the allowed expense for a participating provider. The member, therefore, is not responsible for this amount.

Understanding the EOB

Why did you get paid only $227.20 when you submitted a bill for $410? For the first session, $35 of your $110 fee was "not allowed" since in this example your contracted rate for an intake session (CPT code 90801) is $75. In our example, Jack's co-insurance (the percentage of the contracted rate that he is responsible to pay) is 20 percent, so he is responsible for 20 percent of your contracted rate of $75, or $15. CureQuick paid the rest. Not all plans pay more for an intake session.

For sessions two and four, $33 of your full fee was not allowed, since your contracted rate for individual sessions is $67. Note the CPT code for an individual session of 50 minutes (90806). Jack paid his co-insurance, which is 20 percent of $67, or $13.40. CureQuick paid the rest ($53.60).

You'll notice from the CPT code of the third session that it was a couples or family session. In this case, because $75 is your contracted rate for a couples session, $25 of your $100 fee was not allowed. Jack paid his 20 percent of your $75 contracted rate, or $15, and CureQuick paid the balance ($60). Not all plans pay more for a couples or family session.

The "01" Code in the "not allowed" column is footnoted below the chart, reminding you that as a plan provider you cannot collect this amount if you have a contract with the plan. This would be "balance-billing," which is not permitted when you have a plan contract. You must accept your contract rate as payment in full. The discount is Jack's incentive for choosing a CureQuick provider.

What to Do When You Get the EOB

- If a check is attached, a little jig is always in order.

- **Check it for accuracy.** Underpayments often go unnoticed. Be sure the right amount of provider discount, co-payment and/or deductible was taken out, and that you have been paid the rest.

- If your client has a parity diagnosis, be sure the claim was processed correctly if there is a parity coverage differential. The insurance plan may have underpaid you, reimbursing you at the non-parity benefit rate. For more on parity, see Chapter 7.

- **If you believe you've been underpaid, call.** You can usually get it cleared up quickly on the phone. As always, document the call and representative you spoke with.

- **If the insurance company has overpaid you, call.** The insurance company may have paid more than it should have for a session, or paid for the same session twice. While it's tempting not to report an overpayment, if you don't sometimes the insurance plan may recognize their mistake down the line and ask you for a refund – after you've already spent it. Remember also that it is insurance fraud to accept an overpayment, and you could put your license in jeopardy.

The company may want you to return the check uncashed, or tell you to cash the check and refund the amount. However, in my experience in most cases my call causes them to initiate a refund request. In this case, they ask me to wait until I received a written request for refund from them. One insurance plan had a different approach: since I had other claims I had recently submitted for the client, the refund was taken out of my next reimbursement check.

- **Different claims address?** Don't lose sleep if the insurance company address (usually in the upper left corner of the EOB) is different from the address where you mailed the claim. Claims are often received and paid at different locations.

- **Record insurance payments in Jack's chart,** noting both the date paid and the dates of service each check covered (see sample Service Record, Page 149). Then place the EOB in the chart.

Questions and Answers

Jack has a $250 deductible. Why didn't any of this go toward the deductible?

One of Jack's other health providers (or Jack) may have already submitted claims earlier in the year that satisfied his deductible. Or sometimes the deductible only applies if Jack sees an out-of-network provider. For a client with a parity diagnosis, the deductible may have been waived.

How long does it take to be reimbursed?

It varies by health plan, and depends on how you submit the bill. In my experience it usually takes three to six weeks for the checks to roll in if you mail the claims, but only two to four weeks if submitted electronically or at the plan's Web site.

If you do not receive an EOB within six weeks, your claim (or payment) may have gone astray, so call the insurance plan. Many insurance companies have automated operators or provider Web sites that enable you to check claim status.

What if an EOB combines payments for several clients? How do I file this?

CureQuick may list payments for Jack and for another of your CureQuick clients on the same EOB. It is important not to file this form in either client's chart. This EOB lists the name and private health information of another client, whose confidentiality could be compromised if filed in Jack's chart, where the record could be viewed by Jack or a third party who has access to Jack's chart. You could try to separate the portions of the EOB that refer to each client, and file them in the corresponding client's chart. I have a separate set of folders where I keep these "multiple payment" EOBs, which I file by the insurance company name.

My client doesn't want her husband to know she is in therapy, but she is using his insurance. Will the EOB come addressed to him?

Unfortunately for your client, yes. Copies of EOBs and treatment authorizations are usually mailed to the name and address on record for the primary subscriber (in this case, your client's husband). This is a big problem that to my knowledge has not yet been addressed by confidentiality laws. Your client may want to call the insurance company to see if she can make arrangements for this correspondence to come to her at another address. Or she may reconsider whether she wants to use his insurance, given this situation.

I'm an out-of-network provider, but I offered to collect my client's copayment only and submit the bill for him. But I didn't agree to any fee discount. Why didn't the insurance company pay my full fee?

In all likelihood, the plan deducted your client's copayment and any deductible, and then paid the rest, but only up to the amount the insurance plan has determined to be the "usual, customary and reasonable (UCR)" fee. This is the amount that the insurance company feels is reasonable for a particular service, the maximum the plan will pay for the service given your degree, license and geographical area. But remember that as an out-of-network provider, you can and should now bill the client for any unpaid portion of your full fee.

I got an EOB with an interest payment. How come?

You may receive interest when claims are not paid in a timely fashion. An interest payment came to me from Value Options health plan, explaining "interest is due when claims are paid over 30 business days after the claim date of receipt. A claim paid more than 30 business days after receipt accrues 15 percent annual interest each day until the claim is paid. An additional amount of $10 per claim may be included if applicable penalty payment rules apply[36]."

Why Your Claim Might Be Denied

- Perhaps you had no problem when checking coverage. But once you submit the claim, it is denied. When this happens, the Explanation of Benefits should list a reason. In my experience, the listed reason for denial is often not the reason it was actually denied. Go figure. While you can't always trust the denial reason outlined on the EOB, it is sometimes accurate. A few reasons why your claim might be denied include:

- **Diagnosis issues.** You have given your client only a V-Code, when most plans require an Axis I or II diagnosis (except for EAPs, which allow V-code diagnoses). Or perhaps you may not have used the full number of digits required for that diagnosis by the ICD (see Resources, Page 133). Most commonly, five digits (two to the right of the decimal) are required for diagnoses, though some diagnoses have only three or four digits.

- **No authorization was found** in place on the date of the session you claimed. The client may not have gotten pre-authorization for the visits, it may have expired by the date of the session, or you may have already exceeded the number of allotted sessions.

- **Wrong CPT code.** You billed for a type of service other than the one(s) that were authorized, used a code they do not cover, or used a non-existent code (see Resources, Page 133, for CPT codes).

- **Wrong place-of-service code.** For example, under "Place of Service," you may have written "O," "OV," "OFF" or "Office" to stand for office, instead of the required "11" (for "office"). Or you may have used the wrong code (or one they will not reimburse for (see Resources, Page 133, for Place of Service Codes).

- **Telephone therapy sessions were billed** when this is not a covered benefit.

- **You are not a network provider,** and the plan doesn't reimburse for out-of-network providers (this would occur with HMOs or EPOs).

- **Missing EOB.** If you are billing the secondary health plan, you should have attached the EOB from the primary plan (see Double Coverage, Chapter 17).

- **Déjà vu.** You have previously billed for this date of service.

- **The client has exceeded his or her yearly benefits.** If you feel the client is in need of more sessions, you may want to look into an exchange of benefits (see Page 57).

- **The claim was not submitted in a timely manner.** Some plans require the claim be submitted no more than 60 or 90 days after the date of service. In this situation, the plan may not allow you to bill the client.

- **The claim was not submitted to the correct claims address.** Always check the claims address by calling the plan before submission! Never trust the claim address on the health plan card, or even the one given by the automated phone service at the health plan, as it is often the address for medical claims only, out-of-date, or just plain wrong.

- **You submitted the incorrect claim form or neglected to include the required documents.** The plan might not accept a CMS-1500 (especially EAPs, which often have forms of their own), or may require the new revised CMS-1500 and you submitted an old form. Some companies (EAPs especially) might require that you send along treatment summaries or closed case forms before they will pay.

- **The claim was incomplete or illegible.**

- **The claim is being held, or "pended," awaiting further information** needed to process the claim. Frequently, a claim is pended awaiting information from the member about coordination of benefits. The insurer wants to find out if the client is covered by another health plan that should be responsible for primary payment of the claim (for more on coordination of benefits, see Page 67, and "Double Coverage," Page 106).

- The provider was an intern or associate, and the plan doesn't cover unlicensed providers.

- **The client has a "pre-existing condition" exclusion.** "Insurance companies try to discourage people from waiting until they get sick in order to purchase health insurance. One way they do this is to impose pre-existing condition exclusion periods," writes Kelly Montgomery, Director of Health Insurance Advocacy for the American Diabetes Association[37]. "This means that if you have a medical problem which exists at the time you enroll in or purchase your health insurance, the insurance company may deny all claims pertaining to this medical problem for a certain period of time." For employer-provided coverage, the exclusion period is typically limited to 12 months, and only applies to conditions for which you sought treatment (or should have sought treatment) in the six months leading up to enrollment. The good news? This exclusion will often be waived if the client can prove they had previous health coverage right before enrolling – that is, they had no period of time without some health coverage.

What to Do If Your Claim is Denied

Breathe. Count to ten. Meditate. Perhaps a little yoga stretching. Then see Chapter 13 for ideas on what to do next.

13
Appeals
Fighting Denials

૪ ૭

The Explanation of Benefits comes in the mail for your sessions with Jack. However, no matter how hard you shake the envelope, the expected reimbursement check does not fall out. Upon closer inspection of the EOB, you see the charges were denied. Or perhaps you have requested more sessions, and you receive a phone message from Jack's case manager saying she doesn't see why the treatment is medically necessary. What do you do?

The 10 Rules of Successful Telephone Appeals

1. A phone call should be your first response. It often allows for a better understanding of the reason for the denial, and it speeds up the resolution.
2. Have the client's chart in front of you. Take time to review the case before calling.
3. If the issue involves medical necessity, you might want to review the plan's medical necessity guidelines, often part of the provider manual, which may be available on the plan's Web site.

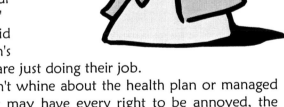

4. Put aside at least 20 to 30 minutes for the phone call. You may need to talk to several people at the health plan in some detail. You don't want to hang up frustrated with the matter unresolved, only to have to call again.
5. Take a deep breath. Use one of those relaxation techniques you teach your clients, and get into your "happy place."
6. Be friendly, stay calm, and avoid defensiveness. Remember: The plan's employees are not your enemy. They are just doing their job.
7. Be specific about what you want. Don't whine about the health plan or managed care as a whole. While you certainly may have every right to be annoyed, the wrong attitude can quickly alienate those who are in a position to help you.
8. If you are talking to a case manager, speak to him or her as a peer, which may be the case — an increasing number of case managers are licensed clinicians. Take the approach that the case manager simply knows less about the client's situation than you do, and with some additional enlightenment, might share your view.
9. Avoid anything that might be interpreted as a threat, such as overly dramatic predictions that your client will certainly decompensate or commit suicide if your appeal is not granted.

10. As always, keep a communication log. Record the names of all insurance plan staff you speak with, dates and times of conversations, and what they say. If they have agreed to resubmit a claim for reprocessing, ask them to read aloud what they have written to the claims department about the reason you are requesting an adjustment, to be sure the information is accurate and clear.

Steps to Appealing a Denial

- **Call the health plan.** But who do you talk to?

   1. **Claims issues:** Call the Claims Department or Customer Service. With your help, they often quickly identify their errors on the phone, and promise to resubmit the claims for reprocessing. At other times, they help you identify your error, and you can resubmit the claim. Be sure to attach a note (a Post-It note will do) clearly indicating that this is a "corrected claim," identifying the correction so the claims reviewer doesn't miss the correction and deny it again.

   2. **Treatment, authorization, or medical necessity issues:** Call your client's case manager. While I think these denials are rarer than most clinicians imagine, they do occur. Usually case managers will set up a telephone interview if they have questions or concerns about your treatment. Take time before you pick up the phone to put together a reasoned, clinical, non-defensive argument for why you believe the services are medically necessary (see Page 48), and why you feel it is the best treatment alternative at this time for this client. Articulate how the sessions might help prevent a need for more lengthy and/or intensive (and costly) treatment such as hospitalization.

- **If you have to leave a message,** leave as much identifying information as possible. This may include your name (spelled out slowly), your area code and phone number (repeated once), the client's name (spelled out slowly), the policyholder's name and ID number, the client's date of birth, and details about your problem. See Page 28 for tips and a sample script. If it is a claims issue, include the date(s) of service in question and the amount you charged, and the claim number, if you have it.

- **If necessary, ask to speak to a supervisor.** Supervisors may have the power to make exceptions to company policy, or may be more knowledgeable about plans or parity laws. They may also assist you if you have a complaint about a claims representative or case manager you have been dealing with. However, don't attempt to bypass the claims or customer service representative or case manager; usually a supervisor will not speak with you unless you have discussed the issues first with someone lower on the hierarchy.

- **Ask for a telephone appointment to speak to the insurance company's medical director or clinical director.** If you have spoken to the case manager and supervisor and have been unable to resolve a treatment disagreement, you may choose this option. I spoke to a medical director only once in the last 16 years, but it was a very positive conversation. He had the power to overrule the case manager's decision, and my request was fulfilled.

- **After talking to your client, submit a written appeal.** If you cannot get the matter resolved by phone, you or your client may use the health plan's formal appeals or dispute resolution process. This is a written notice to the health plan formally challenging a treatment denial or requesting reconsideration of a claim that was denied or adjusted. You may also use this process to ask for an exception to the insurance plan's policies. A sample appeal letter can be found on Page 84. Treatment appeals are then reviewed at the health plan by another clinician, a plan psychiatrist, and/or the plan's appeals committee. You may ask for an expedited appeal if you need immediate approval to continue necessary treatment.

If this is in reference to a denied claim, a letter should have come with the claim outlining the plan's appeal and dispute procedure. Contact the insurance plan for more details about its appeal process, what to include in your letter, and where to submit it. Be sure to file your appeal in a timely fashion. Most insurance companies require that you submit it within a certain time period (e.g., 60 days) of the denial. Many plans have appeal forms and instructions on their Web sites.

As always, focus on why the treatment you provided (or are suggesting) is the most clinically effective and cost-effective. Include a copy of the EOB or any relevant clinical information and documentation with your request for reconsideration. Your client may have the right to receive, upon written request and at no charge, information the insurance plan used to review the initial claim or treatment request. This information can assist in an appeal. You may want to hire an insurance consultant to help you craft a persuasive appeal letter (see Resources, Page 133).

- **Contact your professional organization.** They can often give you advice on how to challenge a denial, or which section of law to cite when appealing.

- **Contact your state's Department of Insurance** (and/or the state's Department of Managed Health Care, if you have one in your state -- see Appendix A, Page 129). Most states allow you to file a complaint (or appeal a decision by an insurance plan) after your complaint has been through the plan's internal dispute resolution process, or if you have not received a timely response to your complaint.

  In addition, when a health plan is denying, delaying, or modifying a service because it does not believe the service is medically necessary, you may be able to request an Independent Medical Review (IMR) from your state's Insurance or Managed Care Department. The case is reviewed by experts in the field who are not affiliated with the client's health care plan. <u>You can use this process even if you are an out-of network provider.</u> Of the mental health IMRs performed by the California Department of Managed Health Care in 2003, 42% overturned the ruling of the health plan[38]. You may be able to request an expedited review of the grievance for cases that involve an imminent and serious threat to the health of the client if treatment is disrupted. In extreme cases, it may be wise to file grievances with the plan and the state agency at the same time.

- **The client may get the employer or employer's benefits manager involved,** asking them to contact the insurance plan on the client's behalf. Only a client should initiate contact with his or her benefits manager – you should not call this person. Once when I was unable to get a claim denial overturned, my client went to Human Resources at his company and spoke to the benefits manager, who was able to get the insurance plan to pay me. Because the employer pays the insurance plan's premiums, the employer often has more clout, and can be an influential ally. While cost containment is important to managed care organizations, customer satisfaction is vital to their survival. They know that if clients complain about their health plan to their employer, the employer may find a new plan.

- **You or your client may have the right to bring a civil action** if a final appeal is denied. Consulting an attorney may be advised.

- **If the service will not be covered, and the client still requests it,** the client may choose to pay you out of pocket. It is wise to have the client sign and return a self-pay agreement (see sample on Page 151). This agreement states that the client understands that he or she is obligated to pay for the services to be rendered, and that reimbursement was denied (or not requested) from the plan. This agreement should be given to the client in advance of providing the out-of-pocket services.

Specific Appeal Situations

1. **If you are not being covered because you are not an HMO or EPO network provider,** you or the client may write a letter to the health plan (perhaps with supporting documents from you and/or his doctor) that states the reasons he went to an out-of-network provider, and the reasons it is believed you are the best provider to see. Insurance plans may pay for out-of-network services when the case can be made that you have qualifications that other providers on the network and within a reasonable proximity do not possess (see "Ad hoc providers," Page 24). They may even pay your full fee. However, even if approved, the insurance plan may not cover sessions that have already taken place.

2. **If the service you provided (or intend to provide) is not a covered service or benefit,** be prepared to give reasons why the health plan should make an exception in this case. Focus on cost-efficiency and effective symptom-reduction.

3. **If your license is not covered because the company is a self-funded/ERISA plan, or because the insurer is an out-of-state plan,** a lot depends on your specific situation, so contact your professional organization for advice. The organization may be able to cite state law that can assist you in your appeal. For example, California Insurance Code's "Freedom of Choice" laws (Section 10176 and 10176.7) mandate that insurance companies may not prohibit their members from selecting licensed marriage and family therapists (and other named mental health professionals), even if the insurance coverage is provided by an out-of-state plan.[39] If the plan reimburses other providers with virtually the same license requirements and training (e.g., a plan may reimburse LCSWs but not LMFTs), you might ask the insurance company to defend its reasoning.

4. **If you are told couples counseling is not covered,** see "Care Denials," Page 43.

5. **If you believe there was a claims error which involved parity provisions** (i.e., your client has a parity diagnosis, but the plan processed it at a non-parity rate), remind the company of the parity coverage benefit. If the plan representative you speak with doesn't recognize the concept of "parity," she may recognize the phrase "Severe Mental Illness" (SMI), "Severe Emotional Disturbance" (SED), or "Biologically-Based Disorder." If all else fails, ask to speak to a supervisor, who may be more familiar with parity laws (see Chapter 7 for more on parity laws). Remember, however, that many plans are exempt from parity laws.

6. **If the insurance company told you when you first called that the client was eligible, or covered at a certain rate, but now says he never was:** In some cases this happens because, when you first called, Jack's employer had not yet informed the insurance company about a change in Jack's employment status or coverage. In other cases, the representative you spoke with just goofed and gave you the wrong benefit information. Don't despair! On more than one occasion I have persuaded insurance plans to pay (even when a client wasn't eligible) when I was able to prove the insurance company misquoted benefits in that first call and it was their error. I had good notes from those initial calls, including who I spoke with, when, and what was said. I argued that treatment decisions had been based on that information. The claims supervisor pulled up the client's computer file and viewed the notes (or the recording) from that call, enabling her to see it had been the representative's mistake. Now you can't count on this, as most health plans give a disclaimer on the phone that says that quoted benefits are not guaranteed, and coverage cannot be determined until you submit a claim.

7. **If the health insurance plan paid for a period of time, then discontinued payment or demands reimbursement,** again, a phone call might be all that is needed to reverse this. Once when an insurance plan suddenly stopped paying my claims, I found out my client's coverage had been terminated. However, without a big fight on my part, the plan said it would "honor the treatment authorization" that was in place, allowing her to use the rest of her approved sessions.

   You may also wish to appeal using a theory of common law known as estoppel. The plan has paid for a period of time, and since the insurance company was responsible for determining the terms and conditions of the contract, you might argue that by their reimbursement you had every reason to believe they would continue to pay, and you and your client relied on this to make treatment decisions. Thus the company is estopped, or barred, from discontinuing treatment once it has made such a "ruling" on the coverage[40].

8. **If the health plan will not cover you because you are an intern or associate,** you may argue that you are working under the direct supervision of the supervisor, that your fees are likely less expensive than a licensed professional, which should benefit the insurer. You could also argue that you operate like the nurse practitioner who provides services on behalf of the physician.

9. **If the denial states there was no authorization in place on the date of service, or the authorization expired,** call the case manager. Often you can get the case manager to retro-authorize (or back-date) a treatment authorization for that date of service (see Retro-Authorizations, Page 54). Then resubmit the claim with a note attached, including the new authorization number.

Tips: *1) If you initially received a denial, but your request for treatment is later approved by the insurance company, it is wise to request a confirmation letter or e-mail.*

2) If you get clearance to resubmit a claim for processing, you might want to ask if they will allow you to fax it in order to speed reimbursement.

Sample Appeal Letter

What follows is a sample appeal letter. This is an adapted copy of an actual appeal letter I sent (identifying information has been changed to protect privacy). In this case the claim was initially denied due to my error – I unknowingly went past the number of authorized sessions AND the authorization had expired prior to the sessions. Despite these oversights, I was able to win my appeal. You will note that I admit my error, list specific symptoms and repeatedly stress the concept of medical necessity. Keep in mind that most contracts do not allow you to bill the client for your failure to obtain authorization.

Barbara Griswold, LMFT
Licensed Marriage and Family Therapist
4100 Moorpark Ave. #116, San Jose, CA 95117
408.985.0846   BarbGris@aol.com

January 31, 2008

To: Appeals Dept., CureQuick Behavioral
Re: John Doe, DOB: 11/23/68
     ID #: 559598678, Group #: 45678

I am writing to appeal the denial of claims for three dates of service (11/06/07, 12/12/07, and 12/18/07) when I provided individual psychotherapy for your member, John Doe.

Due to an accounting error, I miscounted the number of authorized sessions Mr. Doe had used for 2007, and went three sessions beyond the amount allotted in his authorization, and beyond the expiration date. This mistake was compounded by the fact that I did not become aware of the problem until mid-January 2008, after I returned from a two week vacation to find that the claims had been rejected. I immediately contacted CureQuick. After updating the case with a case manager (Karen), she felt treatment still was clearly medically necessary, and put a new authorization in place for 2008. She said she would be happy to retro-authorize the November and December sessions, however the computer would not allow her to back-date the authorization that far. She gave me the fax number of the Appeals Department, and encouraged me to submit a written appeal.

While I acknowledge that this situation occurred due to my accounting error and intervening vacation, I wholeheartedly believe that CureQuick is in the business of providing coverage for their members for medically necessary treatment. I did provide medically necessary treatment for these dates of service, and I am certain CureQuick would have authorized this treatment had I updated the case earlier. Mr. Doe has been suffering from Recurrent Major Depression, and has had several Major Depressive episodes during the last few months. This was mostly due to his ongoing unemployment, financial strains, and his wife's pregnancy and ill health. His depression has inhibited his ability to function at home or to find new employment, due to poor motivation, lack of follow-through, apathy, inability to prioritize tasks, and tendency to isolate and avoid. This has also led to poor self-care and conflicts with his spouse.

I respectfully request that CureQuick honor the spirit of their contract with Mr. Doe (and with myself, as a preferred provider) and reimburse for the medically necessary treatment I provided for your member on these service dates that fell between authorizations. While I understand the need for your authorization protocols, I believe that the client's demonstrated need for treatment, the intervening circumstances, and my long record providing quality care to your members should be taken into account.

Please feel free to contact me for any additional information needed to reprocess this claim.

Sincerely,
Barbara C. Griswold, LMFT

84

Questions and Answers

Is it really my role to assist clients in appeals? Shouldn't it be my client's job?

Don't worry; you aren't being codependent if you help a client with an appeal. In fact, some professional associations have ethical standards that require their therapist members to advocate for the mental health care they believe will benefit clients. Assisting a client with an appeal may even be required by state law.

What if the insurance plan wants to see copies of my case notes for the appeal?

If your client signed your standard release form (or the one on the CMS-1500), he has likely already agreed to allow the release of "any medical information or other information necessary" to process the claims. However, since you may need the client's permission to file an appeal, you should explain the appeal process to him, and you may want to have him sign a specific release if you need to submit case notes as part of an appeal. If your client is hesitant to have his insurance company see these notes, you may suggest he call the insurance company to discuss his concerns about the confidential handling of his health information. Of course, your client always retains the option of paying out of pocket for the disputed sessions instead of undergoing such case review.

I want to appeal, but I didn't take good notes while treating this client. Can I write or rewrite my notes before submitting them?

No. This is insurance fraud. Perhaps if you have no notes you could write a treatment summary based on your memory, but be sure you give the date that the summary was written.

Will insurance continue to authorize sessions for my client while I'm appealing a decision?

This depends on the plan, and on the reason you were denied. When it is a clear-cut coverage issue, it is unlikely. However, managed care plans will typically allow you to see the client (and will continue to reimburse you) while you go through the appeal process when there is a dispute over medical necessity and sometimes if you are asking for an exception to plan rules. This is not always the case, so always call and ask. For a crisis case, seek an expedited review with the health plan, so that the outcome can be determined in a matter of days. If needed, contact your state Department of Insurance for advice (see state DOI contact information in Appendix A on Page 129). Be sure that the client is aware of any financial risks involved with continuing in therapy (for example, if the denial is upheld, the client may owe for sessions that took place in the interim).

If the insurance company requests that I repay an overpayment, and I am contesting it, can I delay repayment while I appeal?

Usually, yes, but be sure to ask the insurance plan for its policy. In cases where repayment is requested, call the plan (or the financial recovery service, if you've been contacted by one) and have your intended appeal documented by them, so you don't get any threatening letters when they don't receive payment.

14

Electronic Billing
With or Without a Computer
ℰℛ ℭℬ

Insurance, computers, and change -- three things many therapists avoid like the plague. Perhaps this is why as a group we have been slow to embrace electronic billing, and to use computers in our practices, despite the many benefits. A 2005 *Psychotherapy Finances* survey showed that only 23 percent of solo practitioners filed electronic claims[41]. In fact, only 55 percent of those surveyed used a computer to manage their billing in any way – a figure that has not changed in the past six years. "What is clear is that mental health professionals continue to be the most technophobic businesspeople in America," the survey analysis concluded. However, it goes on to say that most professional health organizations (including the American Psychiatric Association) believe that paper claims will soon become obsolete, and that in the not-too-distant future, it is likely that insurance companies will only accept electronic claims. This is echoed by Provider Relations representatives that I have spoken to at many health plans.

While many of us use our computers for little more than sending e-mails to Aunt Gladys, this magical plastic box gives us 24-hour access to most insurance plans. In addition to electronic billing, insurance company Web sites may enable you to:

- Check benefits and eligibility
- Check authorization status, number of sessions authorized, and expirations
- Download forms and applications
- Submit requests for more sessions
- Submit claims, check claim addresses and claim status
- Update your practice information and availability to see new clients
- View lists of network providers (to assist with referrals)
- Create a personal statement and practice profile, which prospective clients can view
- Access provider articles, newsletters, and contract information
- Access medical necessity guidelines, appeal procedures, etc.
- Correspond with insurance company staff and ask questions

Electronic Billing

Electronic billing is simply the submission of claims information to the insurance plan via the Internet. But there is more than one way to achieve this goal. You don't even need to have a computer -- you only need to hire someone who does! Here are the three most common types of electronic billing:

1. **Submit directly at the insurance company's Web site.** This option involves filling out claim information (usually a CMS-1500-type form) online at the insurance company's Web site. No special software is required. You need only an Internet connection, browsing software (such as AOL or Internet Explorer), and an e-mail address. Claims are filed directly and immediately with the insurance company, without going through an intermediary. It's free and fairly straight-forward for the computer novice. This is a good option for therapists who like to do it themselves, don't have a large number of claims to file and who work with a limited number of insurance companies. Always print a copy of claims you submit online to keep in the client's chart, and keep a record of when claims were filed.

2. **Submit through a claims clearinghouse.** This is a popular option for therapists who have (or are willing to use) some practice management or billing software. The claims are transmitted from your software via modem to a clearinghouse with whom you have contracted. The clearinghouse serves as a kind of intermediary, instantaneously converting the claims to a HIPAA-compliant secure format, then sending them to the appropriate insurance company. The clearinghouse may also provide reports so you can track and monitor your claims. This may be an option to consider if you work with many insurance clients and/or multiple insurance companies. It is a good idea to contact the clearinghouse to make sure the insurance plans you bill are on their payer list, and that they can receive claims from your particular billing program.

   Sound expensive? Believe it or not, there is at least one online clearinghouse I know (Office Ally) which will submit your claims for FREE, and only charges a small fee if you want them to send paper claims to health plans that are not on their payer list. The program catches many errors before the claim is sent, and can e-mail you with the status of submitted claims. Office Ally even has FREE online practice management software you can use if you don't have your own (for contact information for Office Ally, see Resources, Page 133).

3. **Submit through a billing service.** Here's an option for those of you who don't want to deal with computers or billing: Hire a billing service. A billing service is a good choice even if you have practice billing software but don't want to deal with claims submission and follow-up. After you fax, mail, or e-mail your client data to the billing service (for example, in a weekly log of clients seen, date seen, and procedure codes), the service will format and transmit the claims, and send them to the appropriate insurance company's Web site(s), or via mail, fax, or clearinghouse. One nice part: The billing service will often follow-up on unpaid claims, and deal with many claims problems. Some even verify insurance coverage and benefits for each new client within 24 hours, and track authorizations. Financial arrangements vary: They may offer flat-fee pricing (a set amount each month regardless of number of claims filed), per-claim fees, or they may charge a certain percentage of what you get paid by insurance.

One colleague, Karen Rose, MFT, loves her billing service. "They do absolutely all paperwork for my practice, including billing, tracking claims, dealing with unpaid claims, credentialing and re-credentialing. In fact, I now print on the back of my business cards, "for billing questions, contact..." with their phone number. In this way, my clients contact them directly regarding billing and insurance issues, and I can just do therapy[42]."

What's In It For Therapists?

- **Faster payment.** The biggest payoff is that directly-filed electronic claims are instantaneously received by the insurance company, which greatly speeds payment. In addition, electronic claims are typically given priority processing status over paper claims. For example, United Behavioral Health reports that 90 percent of EAP claims and 50 percent of mental health or substance abuse claims submitted online go to a paid status <u>the next business day after they are received</u>, and 95 percent are paid within 14 business days[43]. This means better cash flow for you. CIGNA Behavioral Health states that the usual turnaround time for payment of online claims is 10 to 15 business days[44].

- **Less delay due to errors.** Electronic billing has built-in alerts that prevent errors, and flags missing or invalid information. If there is a problem with the claim, such as a missing CPT code or an invalid diagnosis code, it may be identified before the program allows you to submit the claim so you can immediately correct it. Other errors, such as incorrect policyholder ID numbers or claims addresses, may be identified within a few days, so that you can submit a corrected claim. This quick identification of problems dramatically decreases the likelihood that your claim will be denied, which means faster payment and fewer hassles for you.

- **More security.** While therapists express concern about the confidentiality of client information submitted electronically, some insurance companies argue there is more security in electronic transmission than via "snail mail." Electronic claims are encrypted (translated into a coded message), so the file is secure and in compliance with HIPAA security standards.

- **Cost savings.** If you choose to file claims directly on the company's Web site or via a clearinghouse, you save the cost of claim forms, envelopes, and postage. And even a billing service may save money for you, once you figure in the cost of the time you would have spent doing all that they will do.

- **It's simple.** If you can fill out a CMS-1500 form by hand, you can do it online.

- **Easy tracking of claims.** You are typically given proof of filing, so that you can prove you filed in a timely manner if the insurance company ever questions this. You can always check the status of claims you've submitted, preventing "lost" claims.

Questions and Answers

If I do electronic billing, do I have to deal with HIPAA regulations?

You bet. If you do any type of electronic billing, even if you simply hire a billing service, a claims clearinghouse, or an employee or independent contractor that submits claims on your behalf using the Internet or e-mail, you automatically become a "covered entity" under HIPAA regulations. Once you are a covered entity, you will need to obtain a National Provider Identifier (NPI) to use on claims, and must give a Notice of Privacy Policies to all your clients. In addition, other HIPAA policies and procedures must be followed, both with your insurance clients <u>and</u> with your private-pay clients. For more information on what this entails, and how to apply for a NPI, see the HIPAA section of this manual (Page 33), or the HIPAA/NPI Information section of Resources (Page 133).

Is buying a billing or practice management software a good idea for me?

This depends on the size of your insurance practice. Obviously, if you have only a few insurance clients, it might make more sense to fill out the claims by hand (though the time may come soon when handwritten claims will be rejected), or go to the Web site of each client's insurance plan and submit claims there. However, if you have a large number of insurance clients, a billing program can be a real time saver. For example, with one click a billing program can take the client data you've entered into the program and spit out claims for a whole month of sessions. And, since computer-printed claim forms are typically processed more quickly by the insurance plan, payment is faster. Office Ally has their own practice management software and electronic filing program which is free to therapists, so you don't need to buy your own (see Page 88 for more about Office Ally, or Resources, Page 133, for their listing).

If you were thinking about buying your own practice management program for other reasons, the most basic set-ups start at about $80. If you are like me and your handwriting is so illegible you can't even read your own grocery lists, a program that allows you to type session notes is worth looking into. These programs are more expensive (good ones average $500-$800). More deluxe programs may include session notes, authorization tracking, referral and cash flow statistics, medication summaries, sample treatment plans, reports, sample letters, practice expense logs, client scheduling, and the ability to send financial information to Quicken, QuickBooks, or TurboTax. Remember that not all billing programs offer the ability to bill electronically, and others charge extra for this feature.

Do all insurance plans accept electronic claims?

No, but most large ones do. For those that don't, you can bill by mail or hire a billing service to bill those plans for you.

Can I get <u>paid</u> electronically, too?

The push is on for the "paperless office," and some plans, including Aetna, Blue Shield, and United Health Care, are now able to pay providers electronically through an electronic funds transfer. A representative from United Behavioral Health Care explained that once a provider signs up for UBH's Electronic Payment Service, claim payments are directly deposited into the therapist's bank account. An e-mail notification is then sent to the therapist, and EOBs may be viewed and downloaded by going onto the UBH Web site.

This is available whether you submit claims electronically or by mail. While this service is currently voluntary, the UBH representative said he anticipated it would soon be company policy to handle all claims in this manner, but that exceptions would be made (such as for low-volume providers, those who share a tax ID number, or for clinicians who don't have Internet access or a bank account).

Where can I get more information about billing software and electronic billing?

A list of some popular practice billing software can be obtained from many professional associations (see "Resources," Page 133). In the Resources section, I've given the names of some Web sites that list billing programs and give links to the Web sites of these programs. I have also listed some other resources for electronic billing, and names organizations with mental health billing specialties. It can also be helpful to call the insurance companies you work with (or want to work with) and ask for their electronic billing help desk. They may be able to give you the names of practice software programs and clearinghouses with which their system is compatible.

15
Clinical Issues and Confidentiality
ༀ ༃

So as Jack's therapy progresses, how will taking his insurance affect his treatment?

Clinical Issues

- **There is no way around it: you will need to spend some session time discussing coverage.** You may need to educate him about issues such as parity issues, network vs. out-of network provider options, coverage levels, co-payments, deductibles, session limits, and that his plan may require preauthorization. Jack may know he has coverage for 20 yearly visits, but may not know that these sessions will be given to him only if his plan determines that they are medically necessary. He also may not know that his visits to his psychiatrist may be included in these 20 yearly visits.

- **Brief emphasis.** Perhaps the most significant way that managed care has changed therapy is the emphasis on short-term therapy, especially cognitive-behavioral therapies. And because insurance is illness-based, managed care plans aim for symptom-reduction instead of the in-depth exploration of personality quirks, life goals, career counseling, character disorders, or childhood trauma. "No longer will it be acceptable for the therapist to dedicate the first six sessions to rapport building," writes Mary Riemersma, Executive Director of the California Association of Marriage and Family Therapists[45].

- **Clients may stop coming when benefits end.** Instead of continuing and paying out of pocket when he runs out of sessions, Jack may be tempted to take a break and restart counseling when his benefits renew. It can be a challenge to help clients make treatment decisions that are not based solely on benefits.

- **Clients may be unable to see the therapist of their choice if the therapist is not covered by insurance.** If Jack changes to a health plan where you are not a participating provider, or if you leave the CureQuick provider panel, he may not be able to afford to continue with you, and might need to find a new therapist. In many cases, this can also mean that Jack is unable to see the professional best suited to meet his needs, or a specialist you would like him to see (i.e. a psychiatrist with an expertise in treating pail phobias), if the specialist is not on a network provider.

- **You will need to set goals that take into account the client's insurance plan and its limitations.** If the client has only a few sessions, and does not have the ability to continue with you after these benefits run out, it is important to set realistic goals that can be achieved in the given time frame. You may choose to become more focused in your work, and limit the scope of treatment to one specific issue.

- **Think outside the box.** While once-a-week therapy is often the norm, if Jack only has 20 visits per year, he may not want to use up his limited sessions within a few months, so may choose to space sessions out.

- **Monitor your negative counter-transference.** It is easy to get resentful about the fee discounts, plan limitations, and paperwork, and take it out on our insurance clients. You may find yourself giving preferential treatment to full-fee clients, or feeling annoyed when your (discount fee) managed care clients discuss their recent luxury car purchases or yachting adventures.

- **Crisis cases may mean more contact with case managers.** It is wise to share any serious concerns about risk issues (suicide attempts, suicide risk, violence, substance abuse, homicide, child abuse) with case managers. This helps protect you in the event that Jack destabilizes, harms himself, or harms someone else. Case managers can also be helpful in suggesting resources. For example, if you found Jack had become dependent on alcohol, you might contact CureQuick to discuss treatment options covered by the plan before presenting them to Jack.

- **If you'd like to see Jack more than one hour daily or weekly, you may need permission from the plan.** Some plans will only reimburse for one hour of outpatient therapy per day, and one session per week, unless prior approval is given. As always, ask the insurance company.

- **If Jack can't afford his copayment, co-insurance or deductible**, you may be tempted to help him out by waiving it. Read more about why you shouldn't, and other ways to help Jack out, on Page 101.

Confidentiality Issues

When discussing the topic of insurance, perhaps the biggest concern of therapists and their clients is in the area of confidentiality. Clients who use their insurance are concerned about

how their private health information will be used, and with whom it may be shared. This is especially understandable since the sensitive topics discussed in therapy (such as a client's sexual orientation, HIV status, infidelity, or abuse of drugs or alcohol) could have devastating consequences if disclosed to the wrong parties. A survey conducted by the California Healthcare Foundation found that 67 percent of respondents were concerned about the privacy of their medical records, and 52 percent were concerned that insurance claims information might be used by an employer to limit job opportunities[46]. In fact, 13 percent of those surveyed said they had done something to protect the privacy of their medical history. These protective behaviors included paying out of pocket to avoid submitting an insurance claim, not seeking care to avoid disclosure, avoiding a visit to the doctor for treatment of certain conditions, asking a provider not to write down a health condition, giving inaccurate or incomplete information on a medical form, requesting care under an assumed name, or asking a therapist not to take notes.

What do I say when Jack asks, "How much of what I say in here can get back to my employer?"

I typically respond to this question by saying something like, "What you say in our session, and even your very presence here, is confidential. It is my ethical and legal duty, one which I take very seriously. This means that even if your wife or boss called and asked if you were here, I couldn't confirm or deny it, unless I had your written consent. And your employer will get no information from me about your attendance or what you talk about here, unless you ask me to release this information. Your insurance company is also similarly obliged by law to protect your confidentiality. No information about the issues you are discussing is released by them to your employer, unless you are a management referral. The health plan reports only statistical information to the employer (for example, how many visits were used by employees), and the data is not client-specific." I would then review exceptions to confidentiality, which are  also in my treatment agreement (see sample agreement, Page 145).

If Jack is uncomfortable with the information release, you might recommend that he contact his insurance company to discuss the plan's policies for the handling of confidential client information. Of course, he may always choose to pay out of pocket instead.

Should Jack be concerned that using his insurance might be troublesome for him later if he applies for future health or life insurance policies?

Clients are often concerned if they use insurance that this may be used to deny them future applications for health or life insurance coverage, or might lead to higher premiums or limited benefits. Clients (and many therapists) assume that paying out of pocket will protect them from this potential consequence. Unfortunately, it isn't that simple.

If Jack uses his insurance he will be given a diagnosis, and as his therapist you will have to fill out certain paperwork about his treatment (minimally a claim form). This leaves a "paper trail" of Jack's treatment, and in the future it is possible your diagnosis and documentation could have consequences for Jack. It particularly comes into play if Jack applies for an individual life insurance plan, or loses his employer-sponsored group health coverage and needs to apply for an individual health plan. Unlike group plans, individual health or life insurance plan applicants go through a great deal of medical scrutiny. He might be refused, or the plan may exclude coverage for the "pre-existing health condition" for which you treated him, or the plan may raise his premium significantly, since he is considered at higher risk for a mental illness.

However, even if Jack paid you out of pocket, attending therapy in itself can sometimes have the same outcome. On the individual plan application, Jack will likely be asked if he ever attended therapy, with whom, and what the presenting problem was. If he answers truthfully, he would be asked to sign a release so that the new insurance plan could contact you, the therapist, about the presenting issues, diagnosis, course and length of treatment. So the outcome may be the same whether or not Jack uses his insurance, though if he did not use insurance you might avoid previous documentation of a diagnosis.

Should I make Jack aware of the type of information I have to send to his insurance? Should I tell him that the plan has the right to look at his case notes?

"I can't stress enough that whenever you bill an insurance company for something, they have the right to see your notes -- even if you're not contracted," says Susan Frager, a former case manager and mental health billing specialist.[47] Any third party you or your client bills has the right to determine the medical necessity of treatment. You may want to inform all your insurance clients about the types of information sent to an insurance plan. You could write a few lines in your treatment agreement specifically identifying the kind of information you may be asked to release (see sample agreement, Page 145). Or you could do it on a case-by-case basis, only informing clients who express confidentiality concerns. You could show Jack blank copies of any forms you would need to fill out on his behalf for his insurance plan, and explain the type of information required to process claims or request treatment authorizations. You might also explain that if he chooses to use insurance, he is agreeing to allow the health plan to view your case notes, if needed, to approve further treatment or ensure the quality of your care. Then Jack can make an informed choice whether to use his insurance. While you could stress that insurance plans are also obligated to protect his confidentiality, he might want to contact his plan to find out more about how it handles confidential data. If he doesn't feel comfortable with this exchange, he can choose to pay out of pocket.

What if it becomes clear that I will need to disclose sensitive information in Jack's case in order to get more sessions approved?

While the client may have signed a release allowing you to disclose "any information necessary" to obtain insurance reimbursement, a therapist should make every effort to protect a client's confidential private health information. Don't reveal any more information than you must in order to get treatment authorized or a claim processed. However, sometimes it will be necessary to reveal sensitive information in order to receive reimbursement or get authorization for continued treatment. It may be wise to talk with the client in these cases about the information that will need to be revealed so he can make an informed choice about whether to allow the release. Again, he may decide he would rather not use his insurance to pay for your sessions. Be sure to document your conversation.

Is the insurance company bound by confidentiality laws?

While laws vary in each state, insurance companies can be sued and fined heavily if they negligently release a client's private health information in most situations (for example, to an employer, or any third party) without a signed release from the client, unless permitted by law.

I have a client who is seeking therapy, using her husband's insurance plan, but she doesn't want her husband to know she is in treatment. Can he find out?

Whenever a plan member who is not the primary subscriber uses benefits, the primary subscriber normally receives a copy of treatment authorizations and claims payments. While these may have only basic information on them, it would alert your client's husband that she is receiving treatment, from whom, and what type of treatment is being received. Even if your client is the policyholder, she will get this documentation, so there is a risk that he might open this mail. This is a fact most clients are not aware of, and can be a significant factor in their decision to use their insurance. I advise telling clients up front if you suspect this might be an issue of concern for her. Your client might want to call her insurance plan -- in certain circumstances the plan might be able to arrange for correspondence to come to her at another address, or help her some other way.

Are there any special precautions I have to take for insurance records?

Most insurance companies require client records to be kept in a secure manner (for example, locked or password-protected). You should have policies and procedures for protecting the confidentiality of any stored or electronically-transmitted client information, or for purging of records in a manner that protects confidentiality. If you are a HIPAA covered entity (see Chapter 7 for more on this), you will want to follow the guidelines outlined in HIPAA for the security of all client records.

16

13 Easy Ways to Jeopardize Your License: All-Too-Common Types of Insurance Fraud

୫୦ ରଓ

Most of us became therapists because we want to help people, not because we are financial wizards. In all our years of coursework, we may never have taken a class in running a small business, or in dealing with insurance plans. Because we may not be well-informed about the financial aspects of our practices, we can end up making decisions that we don't even know are illegal or unethical.

In some cases, our resentment about contract restrictions and discounts may cause us to be less than completely honest in our billing. After all, you may feel, these big insurance plans can afford it, and no one will find out. In other cases, you may bend the truth in a well-intentioned attempt to assist clients, to help them afford therapy.

"Some of these practices have become so commonplace that many healthcare practitioners forget that what they are really doing is misrepresenting their services to insurance companies solely for the purpose of getting reimbursed," writes Mary Riemersma, Executive Director of the California Association of Marriage and Family Therapists[48].

So how exactly do we know we've left the land of trying to help clients, and entered the territory of insurance fraud? Michael Brandt, a fraud investigator for HealthNet Insurance, writes that "health care fraud is deception or misrepresentation by providers, employers, members, or any person acting on their behalf with knowledge that the deception could result in some unauthorized payment or benefit[49]." Note that this definition includes people "acting on your behalf," such as billing services or clearinghouses you have hired.

Here's a quick rundown of some common fraud traps that are easy to fall into:

1. Choosing or changing a diagnosis for the purpose of expediting or guaranteeing payment.

   - **Giving a diagnosis when none exists.** It is fraud to submit a claim giving a diagnosis of a mental illness when one does not exist in order to gain reimbursement. This may be especially tempting if a client (or couple) seeks counseling for issues related to self-esteem, communication, career, or personal growth, but there is no mental illness present (as classified in the DSM or ICD). If you do choose a diagnosis, be confident you could defend it later to an insurance company representative, or in court, if it came to that. Document the symptoms that support your diagnosis in your case notes.

   - **Changing Diagnosis:** It is sometimes tempting to give the client a more serious diagnosis than they actually have when you know this will afford them better coverage for treatment. For example, if you knew that with a diagnosis that is included in state parity laws (such as Major Depression) Jack might pay a lower co-payment or get unlimited sessions, you might think about changing his diagnosis. Jack may even ask you to do this. But this is insurance fraud. In other cases, such as when the client has a "pre-existing condition" clause, insurance may exclude coverage for a particular condition that was present before their coverage began. Changing the diagnosis to "get around" this clause is also fraud. "A diagnosis should not be changed unless a mistake was made in the original diagnosis or unless the patient's condition has changed," says Riemersma[50].

   - **Under-diagnosing:** For example, your client may not want to document his substance abuse, but it could be considered fraud if you instead diagnosed him with an Adjustment Disorder when that is not what you are treating. Why? Because the insurance plan might have made different authorization or reimbursement decisions if they knew the correct diagnosis. Also, problems could also arise if there are discrepancies between your treatment notes and your billing diagnosis. While I have heard therapists say they give the same "innocuous" diagnosis to all their insurance clients, regardless of the presenting diagnosis (or lack thereof), this is clearly fraud, and you find yourself in trouble if this pattern was ever noticed, or if your records were audited.

   As I so often say, never give a diagnosis that you couldn't easily defend in court, or that would make you lose sleep the night before you had to testify.

2. **Billing insurance for cancelled or missed sessions without making it clear that the appointment was missed.** While it is permissible to bill for a missed appointment, you must make it clear on the claim that the client did not attend the session – don't use a CPT code that would give the impression that the session took place. Most insurance companies will not pay for cancelled sessions or no-shows; check your contract (if you are a plan provider) or call the insurance plan. If you are allowed to bill for missed sessions, ask the insurance plan what CPT code to use on the bill or claim. Be sure "missed" or "cancelled" is clearly indicated. Remember that some insurance contracts do not allow you to bill clients for missed sessions; others allow it when the client has agreed in writing and in advance to pay for missed sessions.

3. **Charging insurance more than your usual fee.** In your practice, you should have a designated "full fee" that you charge to clients. This doesn't mean you need to abandon your sliding-fee scale. It is OK to slide <u>down</u> from your usual fee, just not <u>up</u> from your full fee when billing insurance plans. While this is not an issue for network therapists, who have a contracted fee, if you are an out-of-network therapist, it may be tempting to charge insurance companies more per session than your full fee. It would be fraud, for example, to charge Jack's insurance $125 if you have never charged a self-pay client this much – it is misrepresenting your actual fee.

4. **Waiving client co-payments, co-insurance, or deductible in advance.** Jack agreed in his contract with the plan to pay his copayments, so waiving it is a violation of that contract. You may not bill the insurance your usual fee for sessions and tell the client he doesn't need to pay his co-payment or deductible. If your usual fee is $100, and Jack's co-insurance is 30 percent ($30) you can't waive his portion in advance. In essence, this is agreeing to see him for $70 but billing insurance for $100, which is fraud.

   Does this mean you can't offer a sliding-scale fee? Not at all. If you want to help Jack afford therapy (we therapists are all about helping), you might choose to slide your fee to $50, cutting Jack's out-of-pocket portion to $15. But in this case you should bill the insurance plan only $50 per session. Another option is setting up a payment plan for Jack to pay off his portion of the fee. "If you do draw up a payment plan, be sure to enforce it and communicate about it. I recommend even putting the agreement in writing, having the patient sign it, and place a copy in their chart. Don't let the balance become the white elephant in the therapy room that no one ever talks about," says Susan Frager, LCSW, of Psych Administrative Partners, a mental health billing service.[52] A final option: Avoid using insurance altogether and simply take a reduced rate per visit in cash, or see him pro-bono.

   Keep in mind that waiving co-payments in advance is not the same as forgiving balances the client has left unpaid. The latter is acceptable as long as you have made reasonable attempts to collect and as long as the debt wasn't waived at the beginning of treatment.

5. <u>Not</u> **balance-billing the client if you are an out-of-network provider.** While network providers are not permitted to bill the client for any amount above their contracted rate, out-of-network providers <u>must</u> collect the difference between the fee that was stated on the claim form for the session and what the insurance plan paid. Otherwise, it is like billing the insurance plan for a $100 session, and planning only to collect part of this amount, so the $100 was a fraudulent amount. Once again, you have the option of sliding your fee, but you must report this reduced fee on the claim form.

6. **Billing for writing reports or treatment summaries, or for consultations with other providers, using a therapy CPT code.** Most insurance companies will not reimburse for administrative time, training, or consultations and many won't allow you to bill your client for them. Check your contract (if you are a network provider). If you are allowed to bill insurance for these services, use appropriate CPT codes, not those you use for therapy sessions. If your contract with the health plan allows you to bill your client, be sure your client agrees in writing and in advance.

7. **Reporting that you provided individual therapy when you saw a couple, or vice versa** in order to be paid for the session. Let's say you are working with Jack and Jill as a couple, but at one point you want to see Jill alone. Jill would have to be the identified client for this session, and have a medical diagnosis, and you would need to be sure she was covered. She might also need her own treatment authorization. You may not bill Jack's insurance in any way that would give the impression that Jack was present in the session (e.g., listing Jack as the client and using the CPT code for a couples or individual therapy session). In certain instances it may be more appropriate to use CPT code 90846 (family psychotherapy without patient present). Remember, too, that if your authorization is for individual therapy with Jack, but you bring in Jill for a couples session, you may not falsely give the impression on the claim form that you had a session alone with Jack.

8. **Providing a couples therapy session, and billing both partners' insurance companies for an individual therapy session.** Because the CPT codes are different, this is misrepresenting the service provided. You may bill both insurance plans for couples therapy, but you need to bill the primary insurance first, and secondary insurance after the primary has paid, letting each insurance plan know about the other's coverage and payments. You must also inform each company that the other partner has coverage (for more on double coverage, see Chapter 17).

9. **Having someone else sign your claims, or having interns or associates sign in a way that might make them appear licensed.** If your license is not covered under the health plan, you may <u>not</u> have a psychiatrist or covered license holder sign for you. The consequences for misrepresenting the service provider can be severe, including jail time, community service, repaying the insurance company, money damages, and potential loss of license. Interns and associates are typically not covered by insurance, and so should not bill for care without plan approval. If the insurance company does reimburse interns or associates, the treating therapist and supervisor should both sign, identifying themselves on the claim with titles such as "treating therapist" and "supervising therapist."

10. **Billing two insurance companies for the same service(s) with the intent to collect your full fee from both of them.** The bottom line? You may not collect more than your full fee for any given session.

11. **Rewriting case notes before an insurance case review, audit or appeal.** This is equivalent to falsifying documents, and you may be guilty of insurance fraud.

12. **Billing for services you didn't provide.** This includes billing for missed sessions or phone sessions as if the client attended. Another version of this would be billing for a 45 minute session even though the client was 30 minutes late, and you only saw them for 20 minutes.

13. **Changing service dates.** You may be tempted to change session dates on the claim, in order to be covered by a particular authorization that has since expired, or back-date sessions because a client has since lost coverage. Or if you know

the insurance plan won't cover your two-hour session, you might submit a bill for two separate one-hour sessions on different days. However, reporting that you saw a client on a day you didn't is insurance fraud (see more on two-hour sessions on Page 70).

"Do not allow yourself to be misled or manipulated by your clients who convincingly ask for your assistance in reducing their financial burdens at the expense of their insurance companies," writes Mary Riemersma, Executive Director of the California Association of Marriage and Family Therapists. "You are the therapist, the one in control of the situation, and you should be the role model. The costs to you as the therapist can be very great should you be charged with insurance fraud or some other violation of law[51]." In addition, from a clinical perspective, you would be essentially entering into an illicit conspiracy with your client against the insurance company, an agreement which could taint the therapy, and negatively affect the therapist/client relationship.

17

Special Issues
Couples, Families, and "Double Coverage"

೮೦ ೮ಃ

When Jack fell down the hill, his wife Jill came tumbling after him – literally and emotionally. Things have been pretty tense at their household, and Jack requests couples therapy instead of individual sessions.

While discussed at different points in this manual, many of the following points bear repeating here, since treating couples brings up challenges when working with insurance.

Couples or Family Therapy

- **Will insurance cover it?** While employee assistance programs will usually cover couples or family sessions, this is not the case with all health plans, though most do. However, health plans typically will only cover couples or family therapy when the client listed on the claim has a diagnosable mental disorder, and only when you can make the case that couples or family counseling is the best structure for treating the disorder. But remember: it is insurance fraud to overstate or create a diagnosis for the purpose of ensuring reimbursement (for more about fraud, see Chapter 16).

- **Use the CPT code for couples or family therapy (90847).**

- **If a plan does not allow couples therapy,** you sometimes will get a different answer if you ask "do you cover CPT code 90847 for this member?" Or you may request "collateral" conjoint visits with a spouse to treat your client. While these are all the same thing, the latter two make it clearer that there is a diagnosed client. You may be able to argue that you believe that conjoint visits will most effectively bring about the reduction of the identified client's symptoms and diagnosis. Be sure to call and get approval in advance. You may also want to ask if the plan covers CPT code 90846, family psychotherapy without patient present, in case you feel this might be helpful in the future.

- **For billing purposes,** the member of the couple with the diagnosis is the identified client on the claim. If both have diagnoses, either may be the identified client, unless one is clearly the focus of treatment. If both have diagnoses, you may want to choose the one who has primary insurance (see "Double Coverage," Page 106).

- **If providing couples therapy, and you want to see one member of the couple alone,** clearly identify who attended the session on the billing form. Let's say you are working with Jack and Jill as a couple, but at one point you want to see Jill alone. Jill must have a diagnosis, be identified as the client on the claim for this session, and she would need to be covered (by Jack's plan or her own). She might need her own treatment authorization for this session. If she is not covered by any insurance plan, she might choose to pay out of pocket for this session.

You may not bill Jack's insurance in any way that would give the impression that Jack was present in your individual session with Jill (i.e., listing Jack as the client and using the CPT code for a couples or individual therapy session). In another example, if your authorization is for individual therapy for Jack, but you bring in Jill for a couples session, you may not falsely give the impression on the billing form that you had an individual session with Jack. Sometimes, as was mentioned earlier, it is appropriate to use the CPT code 90846, family therapy without patient present, but it is a good idea to ask the plan first if they cover this code.

- **If both partners have EAP sessions,** you might be able to bill the first set of sessions under Jack's EAP authorization, and then have Jill get her own authorization, so that you could bill the next set under her name. In this way, if each family member has eight EAP sessions, you could do 16 EAP couples sessions. It is wise to check with the employee assistance program to be sure this is allowed. However, remember that the intention of the EAP program is for assessment, very brief treatment, and referral. If in the assessment it becomes clear that your client will need longer-term treatment, the EAP program may want you to immediately refer the client to his/her health plan for treatment.

- **Can I see two clients from the same family for ongoing individual sessions?** Some managed care companies frown on allowing one therapist to see two clients from the same family separately for ongoing individual therapy. Some will not authorize it, while others do not have a specific policy against it. If you would like to see two members of the same family individually, and you have a good clinical reason for doing so, contact the insurance company to be sure they allow it.

"Double Coverage": When a Client or Couple is Covered by Two Plans

You are seeing Jack and Jill for couples therapy, and both have insurance coverage. How do you deal with this?

When a client or couple is covered by two insurance plans, things get interesting. This may happen when both have health plans, or when the client with the diagnosis is covered by two plans. Remember: One must have a diagnosis – a V-code alone is not usually enough.

While the process varies somewhat depending on circumstances, in most cases, you would:

1. Determine whose insurance is the "primary insurance" (not sure whose insurance is primary? See "Questions and Answers" Page 109.
2. Collect deductibles and/or co-payments as if the primary plan is the only coverage.
3. Submit a claim to the primary plan. If Jack has the diagnosis, and Jack's plan is the primary insurance, identify Jack as the client on the claim, and use the CPT code for a couples session (90847). If using the CMS-1500 claim form, fill in the details about Jill's plan when asked about "other insurance" (boxes 9, 9a-d, and 11d).
4. Jack's plan will send an Explanation of Benefits (EOB) with their payment.
5. Then you (or the couple, in some cases) may submit a claim to the "secondary insurance" plan (Jill's) to collect for whatever portion the primary plan did not pay. Be sure to <u>include a copy of the primary plan's EOB.</u> Jill's plan will typically reimburse the couple for their out-of-pocket expenses for the session.

6. Remember: The total recoverable rate for the session may not exceed your full fee (for out-of-network provider) or your contracted rate (if you are in-network with either plan). Overpayments must be refunded to the secondary plan, or this would be fraud. You will also have to reimburse the clients for any amount they paid. If you are out-of-network with both plans, you may bill the clients for any part of your full fee that was not paid by both plans (see the examples that follow).

Huh?? Let's try some examples.

Jack and Jill come for couples therapy. Only Jack has a diagnosis, but both have health plans (Jack's is CureQuick, Jill's is BeWell). You determine that Jack's plan is primary (see Page 109). Your full fee is $100. Both plans pay 70% for network providers, 50% for out-of-network providers. Your contract rate with Jack's plan (if you have one) is $67, and your contract rate with Jill's plan (if you have one) is $70. You find out from submitting the claims that both have a UCR (maximum allowable rate for out-of-network providers) of $90. Neither has a deductible.*

	Example 1 You are a Network Provider for Both Plans	Example 2 You're Out-of-Network for Both Plans	Example 3 You're In-Network only for the Primary Plan	Example 4 You're In-Network only for the Secondary Plan
Primary Insurance Pays (70% in-network, 50% out-of-network)	$46.90 (70% of $67, your contracted rate with the primary plan)	$45 (50% of the plan's UCR, in this case $90)	$46.90 (70% of $67, your contracted rate with the primary plan)	$45 (50% of the plan's UCR, in this case $90)
Secondary Insurance Pays** (70% in-network, 50% out-of-network)	$20.10** (The difference between your contracted rate of $67 with the primary plan and the $46.90 paid)	$45** (subtract what the primary plan paid and the primary plan's UCR of $90)	$20.10** (The difference between your contracted rate of $67 with the primary plan and the $46.90 paid)	$25** (subtract what the primary plan paid from your $70 contracted rate with the secondary plan)
Client Pays	$0	$10	$0	$0
Total You Can Collect	$67 (your contract rate with primary plan)	$100 (your full fee)	$67 (your contract rate with primary plan)	$70 (your contract rate with secondary)
Must I be the one to bill the primary plan?	Yes (It is in your contract with both plans to do so)	No (You or the couple can, since you didn't sign a contract with this plan to do it)	Yes (It is in your contract with this plan to do so)	No (You or the couple can, since you didn't sign a contract with this plan to do it)
Must I be the one to bill the secondary plan?	Yes (It is in your contract with both plans to do so)	No (The couple can -- you didn't sign a contract with the secondary to do it)	No (The couple can -- you didn't sign a contract with the secondary to do it)	Yes (It is in your contract with the secondary plan to do it)

* *Note: This information would change when either plan has a deductible – see Page 110.*

** *The secondary plan may mistakenly pay more – you must refund them if they do.*

In **Example 1,** you are a network provider for both plans. Since in our example Jack's is primary, you collect his co-insurance, and then submit a claim to his plan, CureQuick. CureQuick sees your contracted rate is $67, and pays 70 percent of this amount, for a total of $46.90, leaving Jack a co-insurance of $20.10. You may then submit a claim to Jill's insurance, BeWell (you must do the billing, since you agreed to do this in your contract with Jill's plan). Attach a copy of CureQuick's EOB. BeWell pays the difference between your contract rate with the primary plan ($67) and the amount that was paid ($46.90), for a total of $20.10. You are limited to collecting a combined total of $67 (your contracted rate with the primary plan). If the secondary plan pays more than $20.10, you must refund it. You can't bill the Jack for any difference between your full fee and your contract rate with the primary plan. And you must refund Jack for any payments he made to you.

In **Example 2,** you are not a member of either network. Jack's plan is still primary. Because you are out-of-network, CureQuick will pay $45, which is 50 percent of $90, leaving Jack a co-insurance of $45. Why is it limited to a percentage of $90, if your full fee is $100? In this case, $90 is the UCR, which the plan has determined is the maximum payable to out-of-network providers. The couple may then bill Jill's plan, BeWell, attaching a copy of CureQuick's EOB (you may do the billing, but are not required to, since you have no contract with the secondary plan where you agreed to bill). BeWell pays the difference between CureQuick's UCR of $90 and the $45 that was paid, for a total of $45. The good news? As an out-of-network provider, you are not bound by any UCR from either plan. This means as an out-of-network provider, you can collect your full fee by "balance-billing" the couple for the remaining $10. It is helpful to tell clients up front (or have a treatment agreement that states) that they owe whatever insurance doesn't pay (see Sample Treatment Agreement, Page 145).

In **Example 3,** you are only contracted with the primary plan, CureQuick (Jack's plan). However, you will notice the payments are the same as Example 1. Why? Because the session is processed according to the terms of the primary plan. You collect co-insurance from Jack, then bill CureQuick. CureQuick will pay $46.90, which is 70 percent of your $67 contract rate, leaving Jack a co-insurance of $20.10. The couple may then bill Jill's plan, BeWell, attaching a copy of CureQuick's EOB (you may do the billing, but are not required to, since you have no contract with the secondary plan where you agreed to bill). BeWell calculates the difference between your contract rate with the primary plan and the amount the primary paid ($46.90), paying the $20.10 remaining. You can't collect more than $67 for this session (your contracted rate with the primary plan). If the secondary plan pays more than $20.10, you'll need to refund it. You may not bill the client for any difference between your full fee and your contract rate with the primary plan.

In **Example 4,** you are only contracted with Jill's plan, BeWell. Since Jack's plan is the primary, you need to submit to his plan first. Because you are an out-of-network provider, CureQuick will pay $45, which is 50 percent of $90, leaving Jack a co-insurance of $45. Why is the payment limited to a percentage of $90, if your full fee is $100? In our example, $90 is the UCR, which the plan has determined is the maximum payable to out-of-network providers. You may then submit a claim to Jill's insurance, BeWell, attaching a copy of CureQuick's EOB (you must do the billing, since you agreed to do this in your contract with Jill's plan). BeWell will see that your contract rate with BeWell is $70, and will subtract what the primary plan paid ($45) from $70, and pay the remaining $25. If the secondary plan pays more than $25, you must refund it. You may not bill the client for any difference between your full fee and your contract rate with the secondary plan.

Are you thoroughly confused yet?

Questions and Answers

I've looked at your chart and examples, and this is NOT what the insurance plan representatives (or my billing expert) told me, or even how I've been paid.

Right. In fact, I got all kinds of contradicting information (and downright misinformation) from even high-level folks at different plans. But customer service representatives, clinical case managers, and even network managers are typically not trained about these complicated claims issues. Even most claims examiners don't know how this all works. The bottom line? You are accountable for knowing the terms of any contract you signed with the insurance plan(s), especially your contracted fee, and this is the maximum you can collect for any session if you are in-network with either plan -- no matter what the plan representatives may tell you. Just because you might be able to get away with it, doesn't mean it is legal, ethical, or right. If you want to know how these claims should be handled, it is outlined in this chapter.

What do I do if the secondary plan pays me too much, or more than my contracted rate? Can I keep the overpayment?

Wish I could say yes, but the answer is no. "You need to reimburse the secondary plan even though it is their mistake. The error is theirs for not looking at the primary [plan's] EOB and noting that there is a contract discount. It's a frequent error," says Susan Frager LCSW, a mental health billing expert.[52] "This gets sticky and really requires a claims examiner who knows what he or she is doing...and understands the difference between UCR and contracted rate. Often you get people that don't have a clue, unfortunately." Remember, too, that accepting overpayments is fraud, and violates your contract with the plan.

Your examples make it sound like the plans will tell you their UCR up front.

Sometimes they will, sometimes they won't. Why wouldn't they? "They don't want to risk that the provider will inflate their charge. If you call, you may be told only that your billed charge is within their UCR, or is above it. So you end up having to wait for the first claim to come back to know what the UCR is," says Frager.

Let's say Jack is covered by two plans (for example, because he works two jobs, or has his own plan and is a dependent on Jill's plan), which is the primary insurance?

If only Jack has a diagnosis, he is the identified client. If Jack is covered by two insurance plans, and is the primary subscriber on his (CureQuick) plan and the dependent on another (say his wife's plan, BeWell), the plan where he is the primary subscriber or policyholder is considered the primary insurance.

If Jack is the primary policyholder on more than one plan, you may need to check the effective dates. In most cases, the plan that has covered Jack the longest would be designated as his primary insurance. If both plans have the same effective date, the primary plan may be the one with the earliest date of hire (that is, where he has worked longest). But this varies by insurance plan, so call and ask.

What if both partners have diagnoses and their own plans? Whose is primary?

If one is covered as the subscriber or policyholder on his/her plan, and the other is covered as a dependent (e.g., if Jill is covered by her parents' plan), the policyholder's plan will be the primary one. If both are policyholders on their plans, and both have diagnoses, the "birthday rule" often applies. This means (according to two plan representatives I spoke to) that the primary insurance may be that of the client whose birthday falls earliest in the year (not necessarily the older person). No, I'm not kidding. But in some plans, the primary is the one that has provided the longest coverage. Obviously, this varies with insurance plan, so call the insurance plans involved and discuss your specific case at the start of therapy.

What if my identified client is a dependent child, covered by both parents' plans?

Again, this varies by the company. One insurance company representative I spoke with stated that if both parents are the primary subscribers on their coverage, the plan of the parent whose birthday falls earlier in the year (remember, not necessarily the older parent) is the primary. If the parents have the same birthday, the primary plan may be the one who has provided coverage longer, or to the plan of the parent whose first name begins with an earlier alphabet letter! I am not making this up. Some plans may simply have the father's as the primary carrier. However, this might not be the case if the parents are divorced or separated, where benefits are typically first billed to the custodial parent's plan first, and in cases of joint custody, the birthday rule typically applies. Now you see why you must call the plans involved in your case.

If I provide a couples therapy session, can I bill both partners' insurance for an individual therapy session?

No. The procedure codes are different (the CPT code for a couples session is 90847 vs. 90806 for individual). This would be misrepresenting the service provided, which is insurance fraud. This might also seem as if you are trying to collect your full fee from each plan, which is also fraud. You may bill both insurance plans for the same couples therapy session, but you would need to bill the primary plan first, and the secondary insurance after the primary has paid. You must indicate on the claim submitted to each company that the other partner has coverage, as described on Pages 62-63, and Page 106. For more on insurance fraud, see Chapter 16.

What if the primary plan has a co-payment of $25 and no deductible, and the secondary plan has a co-payment of $35. Which do I collect?

After determining which plan is primary, you should follow the terms of this coverage. In this case, that would mean you would collect the $25 co-payment. However, Jack may be able to seek reimbursement of this $25 from his secondary plan.

What if the client has a deductible for either plan?

If there is a deductible on either plan, you should still handle the claims submission in the same way. However, the plan won't pay unless he has used up the deductible. Submitting your claim will also help the client to use up the deductible. If the primary plan has a deductible, you (or the client) still need to submit the claim so that you can get the EOB, which you need if you are seeking reimbursement from the secondary plan.

Are there situations when I can get paid more than my contracted amount with either plan?

No. As you can see from the examples on Page 107 and 108, if you have a contract with either plan, and you have agreed to accept a discount as part of that contract, you may not receive more than your contracted rate for the session.

This sounds like a lot of work. Can I just collect the co-payment or co-insurance from my client, bill the primary insurance company, and leave it to Jack to try to collect from his secondary insurance plan?

As it shows in the examples on Page 107 and 108 you may do this only if you are NOT a network provider with the secondary plan. If you are a network provider for the secondary plan, you must bill them, even if you are out-of-network with the primary.

If you are not responsible for billing the secondary plan, you may need to educate Jill about the process and give her the necessary documentation to submit, including a copy of the EOB from the primary insurance showing what they paid for the sessions. Be sure they get the proper claim form from their insurance plan (or help them fill out the CMS-1500).

This seems incredibly complicated!

You get no argument here. Sometimes, this makes the idea of having a mental health billing service (one that is knowledgeable about this area) very attractive. But rest assured: In my mind this is the most complicated aspect of working with insurance. If you understand this, everything else will be a cake-walk. In fact, if you understand this, you know more than most insurance claims examiners!

18
Life as a Network Provider

୫ ଔ

What's Expected of You

While expectations vary from network to network, here are some expectations I've found to be fairly universal among insurance plans:

- **Return client calls promptly,** usually within one business day. "One of the biggest complaints we get from clients is that providers never call them back, even neglecting established clients," said one network manager I spoke with.

- **Coordinate care with other treating professionals and the primary care physician.** Discuss the importance of this communication with each client. Make every reasonable attempt to obtain the client's signed release, and always record evidence of this coordination of care. This is especially important if the client is taking psychiatric medications, has a significant medical condition or substance abuse disorder, has a major mental illness, is violent, has difficulty following doctor's recommendations, or was referred to you by a medical practitioner. Value Options health plan reports coordination of care is one of the most commonly missing areas in its audits of provider documentation[54].

- **If treating a child or adolescent, coordinate care with parents, and contact the child's school.**

- **Let the insurance company know about any changes** in your office address, phone numbers, specialty, hours, tax ID numbers, or name.

- **Send the insurance company copies of your license and malpractice insurance renewals.** Be sure you do not let either lapse even briefly during treatment.

- **Let the insurance company know if you will be unavailable** to take referrals for any period of time due to vacation, leave, a full practice, or personal issues.

- **Your office must be clean, safe, and professional.**

- **Keep your records in a professional manner, and make sure they are legible and secure.** There are many requirements in the area of what must be covered in your notes, and most large insurance companies will give you a list of what is required by their plan. This may include the client's name and ID number on each page, and your signature and credentials after every clinical entry, in ink, dated, and in chronological order. You may be asked to include demographic data, presenting problem, psychological and medical history, a mental status exam, ICD diagnosis, treatment plan with measurable goals, releases and evidence of coordination of care with other treating providers, and information on past and present risk factors and use of cigarettes, drugs, and alcohol. This documentation is even a good idea for out-of-network providers, since whenever a client requests reimbursement from an insurance plan, your records may be requested by the plan.

- **Don't speak negatively to the client about the insurance plan.** Don't complain about the fee discount, whine about customer service, or in any way bad-mouth the company. In the contract you signed with the plan, you may have even agreed not to criticize the company to the member. In addition, it is not professional, and may come back to haunt you if the client repeats your comments to the insurance company. I once foolishly told a potential client I was not taking new clients from her plan while I renegotiated my fee, which I felt was too low. The client repeated my remarks to her insurance company, and I got a scolding call from the plan the next day.

- **Don't "balance-bill" clients** for fees in excess of your contracted rate. This is a violation of your contract as a plan provider.

- **Don't tell clients, "my insurance slots are full, but I can see you for full fee."** You can't use the insurance plan as a referral source for filling your self-pay practice.

- **Leave emergency instructions on your answering machine or voicemail greeting.** Even instructing clients to go to an emergency room or dial 911 will usually meet the insurance company's requirement.

- **Give advance notice should you decide to resign from the panel.** If you resign you are ethically and often contractually obligated to give as much advance notice as possible, both to the health plan and to affected clients. Most contracts require at least 30 days' notice, but some require 90 days, so plan ahead. Your resignation must be in writing; send it by certified mail and/or get a return receipt so you can be sure the plan received it. I also recommend you give a letter to all your clients who are affected by your resignation, announcing that you will no longer be a network provider, and outlining what this means for them, and what their options are. If you intend to resign but are waiting to finish therapy with a current client who is a member of that plan, call the insurance company and ask to hold all new referrals. You are ethically bound to transition your clients in a professional manner, and to collaborate in their referral. If you wish to continue seeing the plan's member, a few contracts require providers who resign to continue providing services at the contracted rate until treatment is completed or until the client has been safely transitioned to another provider. This isn't common, but check your contract.

Provider-Profiling

In its broadest definition, "provider-profiling" refers to the type of information a managed care company keeps on its providers. However, to many providers it calls to mind the concept of something more sinister: The sense that Big Brother is looking over our shoulder with a clipboard.

What is in a provider profile? The information differs at each managed care company, and the companies don't like to say what information they keep on file. The information may include client complaints and client satisfaction data, clinical quality/outcomes data, utilization data (e.g., the average number of sessions per case, possibly even per diagnosis), appointment accessibility, and the results of site visit evaluations and treatment record reviews.

While this may be a thing of the past, former case manager Susan Frager writes that some insurance companies' computer systems even require case managers – when writing authorizations or closing cases -- to enter a rating of the provider, in areas such as attitude, treatment plan, and compliance with company rules[55]. "There's also an informal sort of 'provider profiling' which goes on among managed care employees," says Frager. As in any company, they talk to each other. This is yet another incentive for being friendly, kind, and professional to insurance company phone personnel, regardless of your frustration level.

Feeling paranoid? Don't panic. Insurance companies recognize that some clients have more severe problems than others, not all clients are going to love you, and even therapists may get a little snippy on the phone now and then. They are looking for repeating patterns.

Audits and Site Visits

Most insurance companies are required to randomly visit and audit (review) the files of their network providers to be sure records are being kept in a professional manner. These visits also allow them to check out your office, your policies, your forms, and your understanding of their plan. If you are not chosen randomly, you may be selected because of a client complaint, a concern about your practice, or because you are a high-volume provider. What puts you in the ranks of a high-volume provider? Value Options health plan' criteria is "any practitioner or facility that serves twenty-five unique ... members within a year[56]."

The good news is that an audit isn't a blind ambush. When you join the network, the insurance company typically outlines what the plan would like to see in your notes, including documentation of assessment questions, diagnoses, medical information, risk factors, goals, interventions, and referrals. Larger insurance companies often have a copy of these requirements on their Web sites, and some even have an "audit checklist" so you know ahead of time what they expect. The company may even give you warning of the audit, and resend the list of requirements. While it is tempting to "clean up your files" (or write progress notes you never wrote) before a site visit, resist the urge. This is unethical, and you could be guilty of fraud.

And here's more good news: You may never get audited, or you may go years between audits. In my 16 years as an insurance provider for more than 20 networks, I have never

<u>been audited</u> (am I tempting the audit gods by publicizing that?). I was visited only once (as part of my application to the CIGNA Behavioral Health panel).

Colleagues who have gone through audits tell me they are not the hellish encounters they dreaded. Perhaps this is because the goal of audits is quality improvement, not punishment. The key word is improvement -- auditors do not demand perfection. For example, United Behavioral Health has established a performance goal of 85 percent of expectations fulfilled[57]. After the site review, the company gives feedback about improvements it would like to see, if any, and may schedule a re-audit to see that improvements are implemented.

Many providers worry about the idea of opening their files to a third party. However, this is not a breach of confidentiality. If Jack signed a standard CMS-1500 claim form, or in some way signed a release of information required when you submit bills, he gave you permission to release to the insurance company "any medical or other information" needed to process claims. As was mentioned earlier, even if you are out-of-network and Jack submits your invoice, he is opening his files to possible evaluation by the health plan. But keep in mind that if you are a HIPAA covered entity, your psychotherapy notes are protected from insurance plan audits, if you keep them separately from your other notes – no matter what the plan may tell you (for further details about the different types of notes, see Page 35).

Network providers may get also get a phone call from the state Department of Health or the Department of Insurance. Don't panic. They are likely calling simply to verify your demographic information and insurance network participation. They are often just confirming the accuracy of information given to them by insurance companies to be sure these plans have been truthful with them, and have fulfilled certain requirements. You only need to return the call and answer a few basic questions, and they'll be happy.

Controlling the Flow of Clients

If You'd Like More Referrals

There are innumerable creative ways to increase referrals and market your practice. Here are a few that are unique to the insurance world:

- **Call the insurance company and ask about your current network status.** See if there has been a computer "glitch" that has kept you from getting more referrals. You may have been accidentally removed from the network or placed into "limbo-listing." This is when you have not been terminated from the network, but you have somehow lost your active status.

- **Is your information current?** Call the insurance company's provider relations or network management department to make sure your contact information, list of specialties, and address is up to date.

- **Check what prospective clients are seeing on the online provider directory at the company Web site.** If the insurance plan has a Web site, find yourself on the provider directory. Are you even on the list? If so, are you listed as "active," or "taking new clients"? Is your other information correct? Also, does the site offer the opportunity to post a provider profile, listing your specialties or a personal statement? Some companies (like CIGNA) allow you to provide a provider profile and personal statement to describe your practice and your treatment philosophy in your own words. I am often told by clients that they selected me due to what I said in this statement.

- **Be sure you are on the list for all the company's plans.** Perhaps you joined the CureQuick PPO plan but were not automatically placed on the HMO or EAP network provider list.

- **Consider adding groups** that insurance plans might be seeking, and advertise them to the insurance plans.

- **Put your name on the list to provide special services.** Some insurance companies will make more referrals (or even pay incentives) to therapists willing to see clients in special situations, such as emergency referrals, new clients who are about to be discharged from the hospital, or those who have been recently discharged. Being able to provide Critical Incident Stress Debriefings (CISD) or teach employer-requested trainings or lectures might also get you referrals. You might also tell the plan if you are available on weekends, a much-needed service

- **When possible, in your other advertising, state that you accept insurance – you might even list the plans you accept.** I have found this to be amazingly effective. If a client is choosing between you and other providers, and already knows you accept her insurance, you may be the first one called.

- **Create your own Web site where potential clients can learn more about you.** It is becoming very common for clients to check out the Web site of the providers in their plan to help them choose one to call. In fact, recent research indicates 70% of people now search for professional services online first.[58]" More and more clients each year are using the internet to locate, research, and choose therapists.

- **Distribute a flier with your practice information – including the insurance plans you accept) to area physicians, hospitals, clinics, and therapists.** All the therapists in my building have developed a central printed referral list, where we can instantly see who among us is a provider for any given network. This has proved a very well-used referral tool for all of us.

- **Get more training.** Adding a specialty to your bag of tricks can increase referrals. Becoming a Certified Employee Assistance Professional (CEAP) should help you get EAP referrals. In addition, one CIGNA Behavioral Health representative suggested that obtaining a Substance Abuse Professional (SAP) qualification (as defined by the Department of Transportation) could increase referrals. Learning to conduct therapy in a second language (including sign-language) might also be helpful.

- **The no-brainer:** Call and ask the insurance company what you might do to get more referrals.

If You'd Like To Halt the Flow

To temporarily stop the flow of insurance clients, call the provider relations department and ask them to put you on "inactive status," meaning that they won't refer to you for a period of time.   When you would like to begin receiving referrals again, contact them to be sure you are again placed on "active" status.

19

Is Taking Insurance Right For You?

ᏰᏇ ᏇᏰ

A Self-Quiz

Here are some questions to help you evaluate whether to join a network:

1. **What are your practice goals?** What kinds of clients do you like working with? How often would you like to be able to see them? Can the population you want to work with afford to pay you out of pocket for this amount of sessions per month? If not, what options do you have for enabling these clients to see you, and how do you feel about the other options?

2. **What are your income needs?** You may decide you can't afford to discount your fee in order to join a network, but might consider being an out-of-network provider.

3. **What is your cash flow situation?** Can you handle waiting several weeks after a session for insurance payments?

4. **Is self-pay-only working for you?** If you have a number of empty therapy slots you'd like to fill, accepting insurance might be worth considering. Becoming a network provider can bring a steady stream of referrals, which may be very helpful in building or filling out your practice. Perhaps you'd rather collect $60-$75 for an insurance client than collect nothing for an unfilled hour.

5. **How do you feel about advertising?** Do you loathe self-promotion? Have you been doing advertising, and it hasn't helped as much as you would like? Is it costing you more than you want to spend? If any of these is true for you, becoming a network provider can cut down on your need to advertise. As a preferred provider, insurance plans put your name on their provider lists in print and on their Web sites, and they give out your name to their members who call for referrals. I currently have no need for advertising, and get three to four calls a day from clients who got my name from their insurance plan.

6. **Are you losing clients because they need to use an insurance provider?** Accepting insurance can mean retaining clients you enjoy working with, and not being forced to turn away new clients who need to use their benefits.

7. **What's your attitude toward managed care?** Evaluate your transference. Would you resent the idea of a case manager calling to discuss a case, or the idea of defending your treatment plan or care decisions? While this is infrequent, it does happen. Would you be tempted to speak negatively to your clients about managed care, your reimbursement rate, and your participation? If you were to have difficulties, are you willing to work through them with managed care staff? Would you feel like a victim of managed care? If after reading this manual you are still very negatively inclined toward managed care, you might want to stay away from participation with any HMO plans, and maybe even any provider networks.

8. **What is your attitude toward short-term therapy?** While it isn't necessary to restrict yourself to short-term therapy, this is the heart and soul of managed care, and you need to be comfortable with this work. If you enjoy doing in-depth psychoanalysis with your client several times a week, working within a managed care framework may not be right for you.

9. **What level of involvement might work for you?** It may be helpful to review Chapter 2, which discussed the different types of insurance plans, and your options for participation. How do you feel about the idea of becoming involved with each type of plan? You might start out slowly, by accepting insurance only as an out-of-network provider, or joining some PPO, EPO or POS networks (which have lower levels of oversight and paperwork) just to see how this feels. Then perhaps you could consider whether to join a HMO network. Remember, you can always resign any network should you choose not to continue.

10. **Are you reasonably organized?** While you don't need to be obsessive or compulsive to be a good managed care provider, organization is important. Bills must be filed in a timely manner, you must track claims payments to be sure none slip between the cracks, and you have to keep on top of authorization numbers, expiration dates, and amount of sessions used. You may also need to keep a folder for each plan, where you keep copies of the contract you signed and any important correspondence from them. In this way you can also keep track of your contracted rate with each plan, and at have the basics of what each expects from you at your fingertips. This may sound daunting at first, but most providers quickly devise their own organization system (see Sample Service Record, Page 149).

11. **Do you keep good case notes and records?** Or at least, are you willing to start? While this is important for all therapists (and mandated by many state laws and/or professional ethical standards), it is doubly important for insurance providers because of the possibility of insurance plan audits or medical necessity review.

12. **Do you resent paperwork?** At the very minimum, working as an out-of- network provider will mean providing invoices to your clients to submit to their insurance. At the most, you may be providing clients with HIPAA privacy policies, statements of understanding (treatment agreements provided by the insurance plan) questionnaires required by the plan, and filling out treatment authorization requests, recredentialing paperwork, and claims. You will also need to keep track of the insurance plan's coverage details for each client, and keep track of EOBs and claims payment. If you hate paperwork, you may choose not to take insurance, avoid HMO networks (or simply those with high paperwork requirements), limit

the number of insurance clients you accept, or only take insurance as an out-of-network provider. Or you might hire a billing service to do some of this for you.

Don't try to fit into a "shoe that doesn't fit." Taking insurance is not for everyone.

Taking Care of Yourself
The Secrets of Managed Care Sanity

I would not say that working with insurance is an easy path. Most things in life get more complicated when a third party is involved, and therapy is no different. However, if you do choose to become an insurance provider, here are a few self-care tips:

- **Balance your managed care and self-pay clients.** Too many insurance clients can mean you are not collecting your full fee often enough. If your therapy slots are filled by insurance clients, you may end up taking an uncomfortable income cut due to too many discounted rates. Also, the more insurance clients you have, the more time you spend doing paperwork and on the phone unsnarling claim problems

- **Avoid reacting to those who bad-mouth insurance and managed care providers.** There is an attitude you may feel from some therapists who have a self-pay-only practice. That unspoken sentiment goes something like, "I'm a real therapist, not a sell-out like you." Or "real therapists don't compromise confidentiality by taking insurance." Another favorite: "Insurance providers don't have the self-esteem to feel like they deserve their full fee." Don't internalize these.

- **If you suspect a client is unhappy with you,** call the case manager and report what happened, so the plan has your side of the story in case the client complains.

- **Consult with other managed care providers.** Having regular consultation is recommended for all therapists, but I recommend it even more for those doing managed care. There are unique ethical, emotional, and clinical challenges involved with becoming a managed care provider, and it is helpful to have the support of other therapists familiar with these challenges.

- **If the fee discount is making you unhappy:**

  1. **Try to negotiate a raise.** While this is possible, it is rare. A 2005 *Psychotherapy Finances* survey reflects that reimbursement rates hardly moved in the 10 years prior to the survey[59]. Keeping provider fees down is the primary way managed care companies control costs and make profits. While across-the-board raises don't come often, some providers are able to negotiate individual raises based on their unique situations. Call the insurance plan's provider relations

department and discuss your request. The company will often ask you to write a letter outlining why you feel you deserve a raise. Include how long you have been with the network, whether you are a high-volume provider, and what specialties or skills you have. You will also want to remind them if you are able to offer special services that the network may need (such as weekend hours, Critical Incident Stress debriefings, employer training or lectures, or conducting therapy in another language (including sign-language). In short, let them know why you are someone worth keeping -- and even paying a bit more to keep. Avoid making resignation threats – you don't want them to feel they are being black-mailed. You may, however, hint you are unsure if you can continue at the current rate, and explain why, without whining. You may want to hire an insurance consultant to help you craft your raise request, and tailor it to your specific situation (see Resources, Page 133).

In the last two years I was denied a raise at two managed care companies (clearly I'm not the consultant you should hire for raise advice). One company told me that a fee schedule above the standard rate might be considered if an employer specifically requested my inclusion, if I was bilingual, could work with the hearing-impaired, worked in an underserved area, or if I was part of a group practice that could offer a wide continuum of services. This gives you an idea of what you might include in your letter (see "Letters of Interest" Page 22 for other ideas of what to highlight).

2. **However, don't pick up the picket signs.** Self-employed health care professionals cannot unionize for the purpose of collective bargaining. We cannot boycott or "strike," threatening as a group to resign if reimbursement rates are not increased. This is considered "price fixing" or "restraint of trade,as it violates the Sherman Antitrust Act of 1890[60]. In addition, your contract with the managed care plan will likely state that you are an independent contractor. Unlike employees, any attempt by independent contractors to <u>collectively</u> bargain with the managed care companies for better fees or working conditions violates these laws. If the health plan can prove that there was some meeting or agreement between therapists to work to increase reimbursement rates from a plan, the consequences can be severe. This is a felony, and the Act states that "...if convicted, you "shall be punished by fine not exceeding...$350,000, or by imprisonment not exceeding three years, or both."

Many managed care providers are frustrated that professional organizations are not willing to fight plans for raises on their behalf. This is why they can't.

3. **Consider resigning from networks** if you do not like working with them. Contact the plan to find out their requirements for resignations, especially how much advance notice you need to give, where you should mail your resignation letter, and other details about transitioning your clients (for more on resignations, see Page 114).

A Final Question

Knowing what you know now, would you still become as involved with insurance?

I am often asked this question. When I look back now on many important decisions I've made in my life, such as getting married, buying a house, starting a family, and even writing a book, I'm glad I didn't know how much work each would entail before I started. Perhaps then I would not have embraced them so fearlessly and optimistically, or would have steered away from them completely.

If I had read a book like this before I got involved in managed care, would it have seemed too complicated, too daunting? Maybe so. But every payoff has its price. Just because something can be frustrating doesn't mean it should be avoided.

Success in working with insurance requires vision and balance. It helps to have a clear vision of what you want for yourself in your life and from your practice, and it is important to balance the number of self-pay, out-of-network, and managed care clients to achieve that vision.

An over-reliance on managed care clients can seriously cut into your income, leave you ripe for resentment about paperwork and fee discounts, and leave no room for self-pay clients when they contact you.

However, as I said in the beginning of this tome, I feel committed to finding ways to keep our services affordable to the people who may need them most. Not only has my managed care participation helped shield me from income fluctuations that can come from empty therapy hours, and provided me with a steady stream of clients, I have found it to be a wonderful way of keeping my door open to interesting and diverse clients, from all walks of life. I challenge all of you who are reading this to find ways to make what we do more financially accessible to a wider range of people.

So I firmly believe that – even knowing what I know now -- I would still choose to become involved in managed care.

But ask me again tomorrow. Depending on the day's insurance frustrations, I might have a different answer!

Endnotes

ॐ ॐ

1. Mary Riemersma, "The Typical California MFT: 2006 CAMFT Member Practice and Demographic Survey," *The Therapist* (July/August, 2006), p. 26.
2. Tami Mark, et. al., "U.S. Spending for Mental Health and Substance Abuse Treatment, 1991-2001," *Health Affairs* (March, 2005).
3. "Fee, Practice, and Managed Care Survey: New Data Shows that Most Clinicians are Falling Further Behind." *Psychotherapy Finances* (January, 2006), p. 1.
4. Casey Truffo, from a posting on *Psychologytoday.com* online bulletin board, June 1, 2006 (used with permission).
5. "United Healthcare Introduces a New Plan Design – the iPlan," *United Behavioral Health Network Notes* (Spring, 2005), p. 11.
6. "Assisting an EAP Member in Crisis," *MHN News You Can Use* (Spring, 2006), p. 4.
7. Value Options Provider Credentialing Criteria Checklist, p. 4 [online], accessed April 7, 2008, http://www.valueoptions.com/providers/Handbook/2006_Provider_Handbook.html
8. Managed Health Network Recredentialing paperwork 2006 (author's copy).
9. EAPA Guidelines, quoted in "Following are a Few FAQs...," *MHN News You Can Use* (Spring, 2005), p. 2.
10. Value Options Employee Assistance Program Statement of Understanding and Authorization to Release Information, author's copy, received April 6, 2008.
11. NCQA Standards, quoted in "Access and Availability," *Blue Cross Behavioral Health Network News* (Winter, 2005) p. 1.
12. "Fee, Practice, and Managed Care Survey: New Data Shows that Most Clinicians are Falling Further Behind." *Psychotherapy Finances* (January, 2006), p. 3.
13. "Should You Pay $100 to Join a Self-Described PPO?" *Psychotherapy Finances* (November 2005), p. 12.
14. "Standards, Audit Tool for Clinician Home Offices Established," *United Behavioral Health Network Notes* (Spring 2005), p. 10.
15. Ofer Zur, "HIPAA Wants You!" *The Independent Practitioner* (Fall 2003) 23 (5), pp. 194-198 [online]; accessed April 7, 2008 http://www.cpapsych.org/associations/6414/files/files/hipaa/hipaa-reasons.pdf
16. Zur, p. 194.
17. David Jensen, "Are You A Covered Entity?" [online]; accessed April 7, 2008, http://www.camft.org/scriptcontent/index.cfm?displaypage=../ScriptContent/HIPAA/CoveredEntity.htm
18. Phone conversation with Michael Griffin, staff attorney, California Assn. of Marriage and Family Therapists, September 17, 2007.
19. "Value Options and Great-West Healthcare Claims Tip Sheet," author's correspondence, March 14, 2006.
20. Legislative Counsel, State of California. "Confidentiality of Medical Information Act: California Civil Code, Section 56.10" [online]; accessed April 7, 2008, http://irb.ucsd.edu/CMIA.pdf.
21. American Medical Association, *Current Procedural Terminology 2008* (Chicago: American Medical Association Press, 2007).
22. Susan Frager, *Successful Private Practice: Winning Strategies for Mental Health Professionals* (New York: Wiley, 2000), p. 133.

23. American Medical Association, *AMA Physician's ICD-9-CM 2007: International Classification of Diseases* (Chicago: American Medical Association Press, 2006).

24. American Psychiatric Association, *Diagnostic and Statistical Manual of Mental Disorders DSM-IV, Fourth Edition,* (American Psychiatric Association, Washington, D.C., 1994).

25. CIGNA Behavioral Health, "Medical Necessity Criteria, Outpatient Therapy," author's copy.

26. Frager, *Successful Private Practice*, p. 152.

27. Frager, *Successful Private Practice*, p. 107.

28. "Four MCOs Weigh in on EMDR," *Psychotherapy Finances* (September, 2005), p. 5.

29. "Billing for Telephone Counseling or Non/Covered/Non-Certified Services," *United Behavioral Health Network Notes* (Spring 2005), p. 6.

30. Brad Lotterman, quoted in *Psychotherapy Finances* (December, 2006).

31. American Medical Association, *AMA Physician's ICD-9-CM 2007: International Classification of Diseases* (Chicago: American Medical Association Press, 2006).

32. American Medical Association, *Current Procedural Terminology 2008* (Chicago: American Medical Association Press, 2007).

33. American Medical Association, "National Uniform Claim Committee 1500 Health "Insurance Claim Form Reference Instruction Manual for 08/05 Version" [online]; accessed April 7, 2008,
    http://www.nucc.org/images/stories/PDF/claim_form_manual_v3-0_7-07.pdf

34. "Billing for Telephone Counseling or Non-Covered/Non-Certified Services, *United Behavioral Health Network Notes* (Spring 2005), p.6.

35. "On-Line Counseling Gains Acceptance among Users, Providers, and Payers," *Open Minds* (March 2006), p. 10 - 11.

36. Correspondence from Value Options health plan to author, June 2006.

37. Kelly Montgomery, "What is a Pre-Existing Condition Exclusion Period?" [online]; accessed April 7, 2008, http://healthinsurance.about.com/od/faqs/f/preex.htm.

38. California Department of Managed Health Care, "Annual Report 2003" [online]; assessed April 7, 2008,
    http://www.dmhc.ca.gov/library/reports/complaint/2003.pdf

39. California Codes Insurance Code Section 10170-10180 [online]; accessed April 7, 2008, http://www.aroundthecapitol.com/code/getcode.html?file=./ins/10001-11000/10170-10180

40. Mary Riemersma, "Third Party Reimbursement," *The California Therapist* (March/April, 2001) [online]; accessed April 7, 2008,
    http://www.camft.org/scriptcontent/index.cfm?displayPage=../ScriptContent/CAMFTarticles/Insurance/ThirdPartyReimburse.htm.

41. "Fee Practice, and Managed Care Survey, Part III: What Clinicians are Doing about Credit Cards, Computers, etc.," *Psychotherapy Finances* (March 2006), p. 7.

42. Karen Rose, posting on East Bay Chapter, California Association of Marriage and Family Therapist's listserve, March 4, 2008 (used with permission).

43. "UBHonline Speeds Up Claims Processing," *United Behavioral Health Network Notes* (Fall 2005), p. 7.

44. "Web Claims," *Cigna Behavioral Health eBrief* (June 2006), e-mail to author, June 13, 2006.

45. Mary Riemersma, "Managed Behavioral Healthcare – Malady or Cure," in *CAMFT Insurance Compensation Manual* (San Diego: California Association of Marriage and Family Therapists, 1993), p. 76.

46. Lynne Bishop., et al., "California Healthcare Foundation, National Consumer Health Privacy Survey 2005, Executive Summary" [online]; accessed April 7, 2008, http://www.chcf.org/documents/healthit/ConsumerPrivacy2005ExecSum.pdf

47. "Managed Care: Strategies for Billing Insurance and MCOs for Marital Therapy," *Psychotherapy Finances* (November 2005), p. 2.

48. Mary Riemersma, "What is Insurance Fraud?" *The California Therapist*, (March/April 2001) [online]; accessed April 7, 2008. http://www.camft.org/scriptcontent/index.cfm?displayPage=../ScriptContent/CAMFTarticles/Insurance/WhatIsInsuranceFraud.htm.

49. Michael Brandt, "Health Care Fraud Affects Everyone," *Health Net Physician News* (Spring 2000), p. 7.

50. Riemersma, "What is Insurance Fraud?"

51. Riemersma, "What is Insurance Fraud?"

52. Susan Frager, "Dealing with Copays," *The Independent Practitioner*, Winter 2008.

53. Susan Frager, LCSW, e-mail to the author, April 8, 2008 (used with permission).

54. "Treatment Record Review Results: Are You Compliant?" *The Valued Provider* (Spring 2006), p. 6.

55. Frager, *Successful Private Practice*, p. 51.

56. "Treatment Record Review Results: Are You Compliant?" p. 6.

57. "Treatment Record Documentation Requirements," *United Behavioral Health Network Notes* (Fall 2005), p. 7.

58. Joe Bavonese, "How to Develop a Money Mindset," *Psychotherapy Networker*, [online];accessed April 7, 2008, http://www.psychotherapynetworker.org/index.php?category=magazine&sub_cat=articles&type=article&id=How%20to%20Develop%20a%20Money%20Mindset&page=3

59. 'Fee, Practice, and Managed Care Survey: New Data Shows that Most Clinicians are Falling Further Behind," p. 1.

60. U.S. Department of Justice, Antitrust Division Manual, Chapter 2" (1987), [online]; assessed April 7, 2008, http://www.usdoj.gov/atr/foia/division manual/ch2.htm.

APPENDIX A
State Insurance Departments
ℬ℃

The contact information below is a place to start to file complaints about insurance plans, to appeal denials, or to request Independent (or external) reviews. This information is from the Web sites of each state's Department of Insurance (accessed in March 2008).

Alabama Department of Insurance
http://www.aldoi.org/
334-269-3550

Alaska Department of Insurance
http://www.dced.state.ak.us/insurance/
907-465-2515 or 907-269-7900

Arizona Department of Insurance
http://www.state.az.us/id/
800-325-2548

Arkansas Department of Insurance
http://www.state.ar.us/insurance/
800-282-9134

California Department of Insurance
http://www.insurance.ca.gov/
800-927-4357

- **California Department of Managed Health Care**
  http://www.hmohelp.ca.gov
  Provider's helpline: 877-525-1295
  Consumer helpline: 888-HMO-2219

- **California Department of Corporations**
  http://www.corp.ca.gov/
  866-275-2677

Colorado Department of Insurance
http://www.dora.state.co.us/insurance/
800-930-3745

Connecticut Department of Insurance
http://www.ct.gov/cid/site/default.asp
800-203-3447

Delaware Department of Insurance
http://www.delawareinsurance.gov
800-282-8611

District of Columbia Department of Insurance
http://disr.washingtondc.gov/disr/site/
202-727-8000

Florida Department of Insurance
http://www.doi.state.fl.us/
877-693-5236

Georgia Department of Insurance
http://www.inscomm.state.ga.us/
800-656-2298 or 404-656-2085

Hawaii Department of Insurance
http://www.state.hi.us/dcca/ins/
808-586-2790 or 2799

Idaho Department of Insurance
http://www.doi.state.id.us/
800-721-3272

Illinois Division of Insurance
http://www.state.il.us/ins/
877-527-9431 or 866-445-5364

Indiana Department of Insurance
http://www.ai.org/idoi/
317-232-2385

Iowa Department of Insurance
http://www.iid.state.ia.us/
877-955-1212

Kansas Department of Insurance
http://www.ksinsurance.org/
800-432-2484

Kentucky Department of Insurance
http://www.doi.state.ky.us/kentucky/
800-595-6053

Louisiana Department of Insurance
http://www.ldi.la.gov/
800-259-5300

Maine Department of Insurance
http://www.state.me.us/pfr/insurance
800-300-5000

Maryland Insurance Administration
http://www.mdinsurance.state.md.us/
800-492-6116

Massachusetts Division of Insurance
http://www.mass.gov/doi
617-521-7794

- Office of Patient Protection:
  www.mass.gov/dph/opp/index.htm
  800-436-7757
- Bureau of Managed Care:
  617-521-7372

Michigan Office of Financial and Insurance Services
http://www.michigan.gov/dleg
877-999-6442

Minnesota Department of Commerce
http://www.commerce.state.mn.us/
800-657-3602 or 651-296-2488

Mississippi Department of Insurance
http://www.mid.state.ms.us/
800-562-2957

Missouri Department of Insurance
http://insurance.mo.gov/
573-751-4126

Montana Insurance Division
http://sao.state.mt.us/
800-332-6148

Nebraska Department of Insurance
http://www.nol.org/home/NDOI/
402-471-2201
Consumers: 877-564-7323

Nevada Division of Insurance
http://doi.state.nv.us/
800-992-0900 (ask for Insurance Div.)

New Hampshire Department of Insurance
http://www.state.nh.us/insurance/
800-852-3416

New Jersey Department of Banking and Insurance
http://www.state.nj.us/dobi/
609-292-7272 or 800-446-7467

- Office of Managed Care Hotline:
  888-393-1062

New Mexico Public Regulation Commission, Insurance Division
http://www.nmprc.state.nm.us/id.htm
505-827-4601 or -4592 or 888-427-5772

- Managed Health Care Bureau:
  877-673-1732 or 888-427-5772

New York State Insurance Department
http://www.ins.state.ny.us/
800-342-3736
Appeals: 800-400-8882

North Carolina Department of Insurance
http://www.ncdoi.com/
800-546-5664

North Dakota Insurance Department
http://www.state.nd.us/ndins/
800-247-0560

Ohio Department of Insurance
http://www.ohioinsurance.gov/
800-686-1526

Oklahoma Insurance Department
http://www.oid.state.ok.us/
800-522-0071 or 800-728-2906

Oregon Insurance Division
http://insurance.oregon.gov/
503-947-7984 or 888-877-4894

Pennsylvania Insurance Department
http://www.ins.state.pa.us/ins/site/
877-881-6388 or 717-787-2317

Rhode Island Office of the Health Insurance Commissioner
http://www.ohic.ri.gov
401-222-5424

South Carolina Department of Insurance
http://www.doi.sc.gov/
803-737-6180 or 800-768-3467

South Dakota Division of Insurance
http://www.state.sd.us/drr2/reg/insurance
605-773-3563

Tennessee Consumer Insurance Services
http://www.tennessee.gov/commerce/insurance/index.html
800-342-4029 or 615-741-2218

Texas Department of Insurance
http://www.tdi.state.tx.us/
800-252-3439

Utah Department of Insurance
http://www.insurance.utah.gov/
800-439-3805

Vermont Division of Health Care Administration
http://www.bishca.state.vt.us/
800-631-7788 or 802-828-2900.

Virginia Bureau of Insurance
http://www.state.va.us/scc/division/boi/
800-552-7945

Washington Office of the Insurance Commissioner
http://www.insurance.wa.gov/
Complaints: 800-562-6900

West Virginia Office of the Insurance Commissioner
http://www.state.wv.us/insurance/
888-879-9842

Wisconsin Office of the Commissioner of Insurance
http://oci.wi.gov/oci_home.htm
800-236-8517

Wyoming Insurance Department
http://insurance.state.wy.us/
800-438-5768

APPENDIX B
Resources

∞ ∞

Author

Barbara Griswold, LMFT
Gives consultations to therapists to answer insurance questions. Publishes monthly e-mail insurance newsletter.
4100 Moorpark Ave. Suite 116
San Jose, CA 95117
(408) 985-0846
BarbGris@aol.com
www.NavigatingtheInsuranceMaze.com

Professional Organizations

American Psychological Association
750 First Street, NE
Washington, DC 20002-4242
(800) 374-2721 or (202) 336-5500
www.apa.org

American Association of Marriage and Family Therapists
112 S. Alfred Street
Alexandria, VA 22314-3061
(703) 838-9808
www.aamft.org

California Association of Marriage and Family Therapists
Great resource. Articles on insurance, HIPAA, fraud, and parity for members on Web site. Knowledgeable staff.
7901 Raytheon Road
San Diego, California 92111-1606
(888) 292-2638
www.camft.org

Employee Assistance Professionals Association
4350 North Fairfax Dr., Suite 410
Arlington, Virginia 22203
(703) 387-1000
www.eapassn.org

National Association of Social Workers
750 First Street, NE, Suite 700
Washington, DC 20002-4241
(800) 742-4089 or (202) 408-8600
www.socialworkers.org

American Mental Health Counselors
801 N. Fairfax Street, Suite 304
Alexandria, VA 22314
(800) 326-2642 or (703) 548-6002
www.amhca.org

American Counseling Association
5999 Stevenson Ave.
Alexandria, VA 22304
(800) 347-6647
http://www.counseling.org

CMS-1500 Revised Claim Forms

Important warnings!!
--Be sure to buy version 8/05 (not 12/90)
--Most online blank claim forms are for viewing only, and are not the proper size for claim submission (won't align in computer of insurance plan)
--Get single-sheet laser if you use a printer, carbonless duplicates if you fill out by hand and want to keep a copy

(continued)

CMS-1500 Forms *(continued)*

- www.NavigatingtheInsuranceMaze.com
  (408) 985-0846
  Buy forms in batches of 100
- **Online claim supply firms**
  Typically sell 1000 forms or more
- **National Uniform Claim Committee**
  Have line-by-line details on how to complete the new form
  www.nucc.org

Check also with:
- **Insurance carriers**
- **Office supply stores**
  (ex. Office Depot, Staples)

Publications

Psychotherapy Finances (newsletter)
Highly recommended. Managed care trends analyzed and panel openings listed. Marketing tips, financial advice.
14255 U.S. Highway 1, Ste. 286
Juno Beach, FL 33408
(800) 869-8450
www.psyfin.com

Successful Private Practice: Winning Strategies for Mental Health Professionals (book) by Susan Frager, LCSW (Wiley, 2000)
Ignore the title: It is solely a book about managed care. Somewhat out of date, but very readable, detailed, and helpful. Author is a former case manager and mental health billing specialist.

Practice/Billing Resources

Psych Administrative Partners
Owned by Susan Frager, a mental health billing expert (clients nationwide). No need for software: She will submit claims, do most paperwork, verify benefits, and consults on insurance/billing issues.
(636) 464-8422
www.psychadminpartners.com

Benet Clinical Assessment
Listing of (and links to) major billing and practice management software vendors.
9141 SW 49th Place
Gainesville, FL 32608
(352) 375-2545
www.assessmentpsychology.com/practicesoftware.htm#links

Office Ally/PracticeMate
FREE submission of claims to insurance plans, FREE online practice billing system.
32356 S. Coast Highway
Laguna Beach, CA 92651
(949) 464-9129
www.officeally.com

PsychBiller
Website has list of billing software
P.O. Box 2029
Centreville, VA 20122
(866) 475-8612
www.psychbiller.com

California Assn. of Marriage & Family Therapists
Members can get (or download) list of billing software programs.
7901 Raytheon Road
San Diego, CA 92111
(888) 292-2638
www.camft.org

Parity Laws

Your state Department of Insurance

National Alliance on Mental Illness
Colonial Place Three
2107 Wilson Blvd., Suite 300
Arlington, VA 22201-3042
(800) 950-6264
www.nami.org

National Mental Health Association
2000 N. Beauregard St., 6th Floor
Alexandria, VA 22311
(800) 969-6642
www.nmha.org (search "parity")

ICD, CPT, and Place of Service Codes

ICD codes are included in newer versions of the APA's *Diagnostic and Statistical Manual of Mental Disorders.* ICD/CPT/POS codes are available free from many professional associations.

Place of Service Codes (POS)
www.cms.hhs.gov/MedHCPCSGenInfo/Downloads/Place_of_Service.pdf

ICD (International Classification of Diseases)
American Medical Association
515 N. State Street
Chicago, IL 60610
(800) 621-8335
www.ama-assn.org

Current Procedural Terminology Codes (CPT)
American Medical Association
515 N. State Street
Chicago, IL 60610
(800) 621-8335
www.ama-assn.org

HIPAA Resources

U.S. Department of Health and Human Services
200 Independence Avenue, SW
Washington, D.C. 20201
 (866) 627-7748 (HIPAA toll-free)
www.hhs.gov/ocr/hipaa

Ctr. for Medicare & Medicaid Services
7500 Security Boulevard
Baltimore, MD 21244
(877) 267-2323
www.cms.hhs.gov/EducationMaterials/02_HIPAAMaterials.asp#TopOfPage

National Provider Identifier

- **National Plan and Provider Enumeration System (NPPES)**
  Apply for your NPI here
  P.O. Box 6059
  Fargo, ND 58108-6059
  (800) 465-3203
  https://nppes.cms.hhs.gov/NPPES

- **Centers for Medicare & Medicaid Services**
  7500 Security Boulevard
  Baltimore, MD 21244
  (877) 267-2323
  www.cms.hhs.gov/NationalProvidentStand/

Managed Care Company Lists

Many professional associations or state Departments of Insurance have a list of plans that operate in your state.

Fran Wickner, PhD, MFT
Sells list of over 60 plans that operate in California, with contact numbers.
1350-A Solano Avenue Suite #4
Albany, CA 94706
(510) 527-4011
www.franwickner.com

Employer Identification Numbers

- **Warning**: When starting to use an EIN (so that you no longer have to use your Social Security Number on claims) you will need to submit a completed IRS Form W-9 to each plan. Be sure to follow up with the plans or your claims may be denied if they do not recognize your new Tax ID number.

Internal Revenue Service
Apply for EINs online, by phone, or fax
(800) 829-4933 (phone)
Fax IRS Form SS-4 to your local IRS office
www.irs.gov/businesses/small/article/0,,id=98350,00.html

Insurance Consultants

Barbara Griswold, MFT
4100 Moorpark Ave. #116
San Jose, CA 95117
(408) 985-0846
www.navigatingtheinsurancemaze.com

(continued)

Insurance Consultants *(continued)*

Susan Frager, LCSW
Psych Administrative Partners
(636) 464-8422
www.psychadminpartners.com

Fran Wickner, PhD, MFT
1350-A Solano Avenue Suite #4
Albany, CA 94706
(510) 527-4011
www.franwickner.com

Re-credentialing

Council for Affordable Quality Healthcare (CAQH)
Fill out practice information on one Web site, have it sent to multiple plans.
601 Pennsylvania Avenue, NW
South Building, Suite 500
Washington, DC 20004
(888) 599-1771
www.caqh.org/about.php

Resources for the Uninsured

Foundation for Health Coverage Education – U.S. Uninsured Help Line
Helps clients find low-cost insurance, and resources for special eligibility situations.
800-234-1317
www.coverageforall.org

California Major Risk Medical Insurance Program
Helps uninsured find a plan, especially those who have this difficulty because of a health/mental health diagnoses.
P.O. Box 2769
Sacramento, CA 95812-2769
(800) 289-6574
www.mrmib.ca.gov/

Appendix C
Parity Laws
As of 2007

ᏽ ᏽ

For an explanation of parity laws, see Chapter 7. For the latest updates on mental health parity, contact your state Insurance Department (see Page 129), or the National Alliance on Mental Illness at http://www.nami.org (see Resources, Page 133).

Comprehensive Parity Laws
In these states, equal coverage is provided for a broad range of mental health conditions, including substance abuse disorders. Does not exempt significant policy groups.

Connecticut
Includes substance abuse
Maryland
Includes substance abuse

Minnesota
Limited to HMOs only; mandated if offered for individuals and groups
Oregon
Includes substance abuse
Vermont

Broad-Based Parity
In these states, equal coverage is provided for of a broad range of mental health conditions. May include some limitations or exemptions.

Indiana
Includes substance abuse for those with mental illnesses
Kentucky
Includes substance abuse

Maine
Includes substance abuse
New Mexico
Rhode Island
Washington

Limited Parity Laws
In these states, parity is limited to a specific list of mental health conditions and/or excludes equal coverage for significant policy groups. May also limit equal coverage to certain durational/ financial limits. Allows plans to opt out of parity due to cost increase provisions.

Arkansas
Includes substance abuse
California
Includes children
Colorado
Includes substance abuse
Delaware
Includes substance abuse

Hawaii
Idaho
State employees only; includes children
Illinois
Iowa
Louisiana

(continued on next page)

Limited Parity Laws *(continued)*

Massachusetts
*Includes children and substance abuse
treatment for those with mental illnesses*
Montana
Nevada
New Hampshire
New Jersey
New York
Includes children
North Carolina
Ohio

Oklahoma
South Carolina
State employee plans include substance abuse
South Dakota
Tennessee
Texas
Utah
Virginia
Includes substance abuse
West Virginia
Includes substance abuse

Mandated if Offered
*Requires that mental health overage be equal to other medical conditions if the plan offers
mental health coverage.*

Arizona
Minnesota
*For group and individual plans;
comprehensive for HMOs*

Nebraska

Mandated Offering
*Requires a plan to offer an option of mental health coverage that is equal to coverage for
other medical conditions.*

Alabama
Georgia
Includes substance abuse
Missouri

*Limits out-of-pocket expenses; allows
different co-pays, deductibles, and co-
insurance*

No Parity – But Have Minimum Mandated Benefit
*Mandates minimum mental health coverage that is not required to be equal to other
medical conditions.*

Kansas
Minimum mandated benefit if offered
North Dakota

Pennsylvania
Includes children
Washington D.C
Wisconsin

No Mental Health Parity Laws
In these states there is no requirement for parity. May have minimum mandated benefit.

Alaska
Florida
Michigan

Mississippi
Wyoming

Source: National Alliance on Mental Illness Web site (http://www.nami.org), accessed March 2008

APPENDIX D
Glossary

୫୦ ଓଃ

Account: An agreement a managed care company may have with an employer, union, or government. A care management team at the insurance company may be devoted to one account or employer group.

Ad hoc: When a health plan is unable to provide a network clinician in the client's area who is able to provide the necessary treatment, an out-of-network provider may be able to sign a contract with the health plan to provide services on a single-case basis.

Appeal: A process available to clients, their family members, their treating providers, or their representatives to request reconsideration of a previous denial of claim reimbursement, or previous denied request for a covered service or authorization for service (see Sample Appeal Letter, Page 84).

Audit: A review of a therapist's file on a particular client or group of clients by the health plan in order to assure quality of care and to be sure therapist is following insurance procedures.

Authorization: See Pre-authorization

Balance-billing: When a provider charges the client for the difference between the provider's usual fee and the amount the insurance company pays. The client cannot be billed for the portion a network provider has agreed to write off as part of his or her network discount.

Behavioral health care: Services for the assessment and treatment of mental health and/or substance abuse issues.

Benefit year: The coverage period, usually 12 months long, that is used for administration of a health benefits plan. Clients, for example, may have benefits for 20 sessions from January 1 through December 31 of any year, or they may have 20 sessions between July 1 of one year and June 30 of the next year.

Benefits: The portion of costs of services paid by a health plan. If the plan pays the remainder of a bill after an office co-payment is made, the amount the plan paid is the benefit.

Care manager: See Case manager

Carrier: An insurance company is often referred to as the insurance carrier.

Carve-out: When a health insurance company has decided not to manage the mental health benefits for their members, and have instead "carved out" their mental health benefits, by signing a contract with another company to handle the mental health case management and/or claims payment.

Case manager: Case managers work for the insurance company, reviewing clients' care to make sure it is delivered in the most cost-effective manner. They authorize treatment requests and make network referrals when needed.

CEAP: see Certified Employee Assistance Provider

Certification: See Precertification

Certified Employee Assistance Provider (CEAP): A health care professional who has gone through the additional training classes required to become a Certified Employee Assistance Provider.

CHAMPUS (Civilian Health and Medical Program of the Uniformed Services): A medical benefits program provided by the federal government.

Claim: A request for payment made to the health insurance plan from the client or the treating provider.

CMS-1500 (Centers for Medicare and Medicaid Services Form 1500): Formerly known as the HCFA-1500, this is a claim form – revised in July 2006 – that is accepted by many private and federal health insurance plans.

COBRA (Consolidated Omnibus Budget Reconciliation Act): A federal statute that requires employers to continue to offer coverage to employees and dependents who would otherwise have lost their insurance coverage for reasons specified in the statute (for example, loss of a job, disability, divorce, loss of dependent child status, employee death, etc.). They are given the opportunity to purchase the same health benefits the employer provides to its remaining employees. Continuation of coverage is limited (usually 18 months for employees and dependents who would otherwise lose coverage due to loss of employment or work hour reduction, 29 months for disability-related events, or 36 months for dependents who would lose coverage for other reasons).

Co-insurance: The percentage of the fee that a client is responsible to pay (after his or her deductible has been met, if any). For example, if the health insurance company pays 80 percent of the claim, the client's co-insurance is 20 percent.

Continuity of care: When a client switches insurance plans, and the health plan allows (or is required by law to allow) clients to complete their care with their current healthcare provider, or to help them make a smooth transition to a network provider at their new insurance plan. This term is also used to refer to continuing care from one level of treatment to another, such as from inpatient to outpatient care.

Contract (subscriber's): A legal agreement between a member and the insurance plan that describes the benefits and limitations of the coverage.

Contract (provider's): A legal agreement between an individual treating provider and the insurance plan outlining the terms of their agreement to provide services to covered members.

Contracted rate, or contracted fee: The fee the insurance company will pay for a session, as outlined in the provider contract. This is usually a discounted fee from the provider's usual full fee.

Coordination of benefits (COB): When a client has two or more insurance plans, the plans will coordinate the payment of the claim to prevent overpayment/duplication.

Co-payment (co-pay): The fixed, flat fee per visit that a client must pay, sometimes after the deductible is met for eligible expenses. The health insurance company pays the rest.

Coverage: The benefits provided by the insurance plan.

Covered services: Those procedures the insurance company agrees to pay under the member's benefit contract. Most health insurance plans have limitations on their coverage.

CPT codes: The physician's Current Procedural Terminology codes, published by the American Medical Association, were developed to provide a universal language to describe medical and diagnostic services provided by health care providers.

Credentialing: A process used by a managed care company in which a health care provider's credentials are reviewed and matched against the credentials required to participate in the provider network.

Date of service (DOS): The date the service or session was provided to the client.

Deductible: The dollar amount that a client must pay yearly for eligible health services before his or her health plan begins paying. For example, a client with a $200 deductible will have to pay the first $200 of medical bills each year; after that, insurance begins to cover the expenses. Not all plans have deductibles.

Dependent: A person eligible for coverage under an employee benefits plan because of that person's relationship to an employee. Spouses, children, and adopted children are often eligible for dependent coverage.

Dispute: A provider's written notice to the insurance company challenging, appealing, or requesting reconsideration of a claim that has been denied, adjusted, or contested, or disputing a request for reimbursement of an overpayment of a claim.

Dispute resolution: The process that each insurance company has set up for handling and settling disputes.

DOS: See Date of service

Double (or Duplicate) coverage: When a client has coverage for the same health services under more than one health benefits plan (e.g., he is covered by insurance through both his employer and his wife's employer).

EAP: See Employee assistance program, or employee assistance provider/professional.

EIN (Employer Identification Number): This is a type of Tax Identification Number (TIN) that any business (including therapists in private practice) can obtain from the Internal Revenue Service. The EIN can be used on claims and invoices in place of your Social Security Number.

Effective date: The date on which the client's coverage began under the health benefits plan.

Eligible services: Services are considered eligible or ineligible for coverage by the health benefits plan depending on the plan's provisions.

Employee assistance professional/provider (EAP): A clinician who has contracted with an employee assistance program to provide counseling services which are free to the employee or dependent.

Employee assistance program (EAP): An EAP is an assessment, referral and short-term counseling program that is pre-purchased by some employers and is available for free to their employees and dependents. An employer may hire EAP professionals that work on-site at the company, or may contract with clinicians in the community.

Employee Retirement Income Security Act (ERISA): A federal law that applies to retirement programs and to employee welfare benefit programs established or maintained by employers and unions. Because these plans are governed by ERISA, which is federal law, the federal law pre-empts state law, and thus self-insured benefit plans can avoid state mandates, such as parity laws.

Employer Identification Number: see EIN

Enrollee: An individual who is enrolled and eligible for coverage under a health plan.

EOB: See Explanation of benefits.

EPO (exclusive provider organization): A specific type of health plan similar to a PPO, except that the client does not have the option of choosing an out-of-network provider for reimbursable services. Plan members can visit specialists without a referral, and don't need to choose a primary care physician for coverage.

ERISA: See Employee Retirement Income Security Act

Exclusions: Specific conditions or services that are not covered under the benefit agreement.

Exclusive provider organization: See EPO

Explanation of benefits (EOB): Once a claim is made for services, an EOB is the statement provided by the health plan that accompanies the reimbursement check, and explains how the claim was processed. It may include the portion of the charges that went to satisfy the client's deductible or co-insurance, and any other adjustments made before it was paid. Or it may explain why the claim was not paid. A copy of the EOB goes to both the insured and the provider.

Fee-for-service plans: A healthcare plan in which providers receive payment based on their billed charges for each service provided without treatment review or authorization. These plans are not considered "managed care," and allow visits to any healthcare professional. See Indemnity plans.

Flexible spending account (FSA): An employer-sponsored tax-advantaged savings account that clients may use to pay medical and dependent care expenses. Clients must designate in advance how much they want to put in the account that year, and if it is not spent by year-end, it is lost.

GAF (Global Assessment of Functioning): Part of the diagnostic system as outlined in the *Diagnostic and Statistical Manual of Mental Disorders* (DSM-IV), this is Axis 5, which gives therapists a 1-100 scale upon which to rate their client's functioning. Insurance companies may use this to measure progress.

HCFA-1500: See CMS 1500.

Health Insurance Portability and Accountability Act: see HIPAA

Health maintenance organization: See HMO

Health reimbursement account (HRA): These are tax-exempt accounts that many employers have paid into that employees may use specifically for the payment of health care expenses. Clients control the investments they make, the amount they deposit, and what expenses they pay.

Health savings account (HSA): These are tax-exempt accounts that many clients (and often their employers) have paid into that employees may use for the payment of health care expenses. Clients control the investments they make, the amount they deposit, and what expenses they pay. They are also required to have a high deductible health plan.

HIPAA (Health Insurance Portability and Accountability Act): This law addresses health insurance portability, and is designed to protect health insurance coverage for workers and their families when they change or lose their jobs. It is also aimed at reducing the administrative costs of providing health care through standardization, and includes requirements to protect the privacy of clients' health information. Health plans and many providers who transmit confidential health information electronically are required to follow the requirements of HIPAA.

HMO (health maintenance organization): A health plan that typically offers broader preventive coverage and lower out-of-pocket expenses for its members. Plan members are required to have a primary care physician, who coordinates care, and his/her referral is usually required to see specialists. There is typically no annual deductible, and co-payments are usually low. However, coverage is not available for out-of-network providers, except for emergency care.

HRA: See Health reimbursement arrangement

HSA: See Health savings account

ICD (International Classification of Diseases): Diagnostic codes developed by the American Medical Association, and now required by health insurers on claim forms.

Indemnity plan: A type of health benefits plan under which the covered person pays an annual deductible, and then the health benefit plan pays a percentage of covered charges. No primary care physician referral is required, no referrals are required for specialists, and there are no provider networks. The provider controls the type of treatment, length of treatment, and fee charged. Also called a fee-for-service plan.

Insured: The individual who is enrolled and eligible for coverage under a health plan.

Invoice: A list of charges and payments made for healthcare services provided. This may be given to a client to submit to their insurance plan for reimbursement. Also known as a statement or Superbill (see sample invoice Page 147).

Legacy Identifiers: Before the advent of the National Provider Identifier (NPI), these were the identification numbers used by a health plan to identify a particular provider. Examples include Provider Identification Numbers (PINS), Unique Physician Identification Numbers (UPINs) and state license numbers. Legacy Identifiers may still be accepted on claim forms by some insurance plans if a provider is not a HIPAA Covered Entity, in which case the provider is required to use an NPI (see section on HIPAA, Page 33).

Lifetime maximum/limit: The cap on the benefits paid under an insurance policy during a client's lifetime.

Managed care: A system of health care delivery that is designed to manage the cost, use and quality of the health care, and typically offers financial incentives for clients to use the providers who belong to the plan. Managed care may include pretreatment authorization, utilization review, and provider discounts. Examples include HMO, PPO, EPO, and POS plans.

Medical necessity: The health plan's determination that there is a medical need for treatment, that the course of treatment is the most appropriate for the symptoms the client is experiencing, is provided within generally accepted standards of practice, and is not rendered primarily for the convenience of the client or provider.

Medical savings account (MSA): See Health savings account

Member: The individual or dependent who is enrolled in and eligible for coverage under a health plan.

MH/SA: An abbreviation used by insurers to refer to Mental Health and Substance Abuse benefits.

National Provider Identifier (NPI): As part of HIPAA laws, The Centers for Medicare and Medicaid Services (CMS) will be assigning all HIPAA providers ("covered entities") unique provider identification numbers to use when billing and communicating with all private and government health plans.

Network: A group of health care providers under contract with a managed care company. They may agree to accept discounts, file claims, and permit their treatment to be reviewed.

Network provider: Any health care provider who has entered into an agreement with a managed care plan, and thus belongs to the insurance plan's network of providers. Choosing a network provider gives the member the advantage of discounted fees, and often better coverage by the health plan. Also called a participating provider.

NPI: see National Provider Identifier

Open enrollment: A period when eligible persons can enroll in a new health benefit plan for the next benefit year.

Out-of-network provider: Any health care provider that does not belong to the insurance plan's network. Many insurance plans cover visits to out-of-network providers, but often at a lower reimbursement rate.

Out-of-pocket expenses: Co-payments, deductibles, or fees paid by clients for health services.

Out-of-pocket maximum: The most money a client will be required to pay per year for deductibles and co-insurance payments before the plan begins to pay 100 percent of covered health expenses. This does not include the payment of regular premiums.

Panel: The network of providers who have contracted with a health care plan to provide services to the insurance members or enrollees. Also known as the provider network.

Parity: A series of federal and state laws which require insurance companies to grant some measure of equality between mental health and medical benefits.

Participant: A person who is eligible to receive health benefits under a health benefits plan. This may refer to the employee, spouse, or other dependents.

Participating provider: Any health care provider that has entered into an agreement with a managed care plan, and thus belongs to the insurance plan's network of providers. Choosing a participating provider (network provider) gives the member the advantage of discounted fees, and often better coverage by the health plan. Also called a network provider.

Pass-through: Some health plans allow a certain number of visits with a provider before authorization for treatment is needed. These are called "pass-through sessions."

Payer: An insurance company, self-funded employer, union or employer trust, managed care plan, state or federal government agency which has entered into a contractual arrangement to pay for health services.

PCP: See Primary care physician

Pended claim: A claim that has been delayed because it requires additional information before it can be processed. This often involves waiting for information about whether the client has a second insurance plan covering him or her.

Place-of-service code: See POS code

Plan: An employee benefits arrangement offered by an insurance company so that health care services are provided to covered members or enrollees in the plan.

Point-of-service plan: See POS

Policyholder: The individual to whom an insurance contract is issued, usually the employee in an employer-sponsored health plan.

Portability: The ability for an individual to transfer from one health insurance plan to another (including after a change of job status, or change of plans offered by the employer) and still be covered.

POS (Place-of-service) code: This code, placed on a claim form, informs insurance companies where the treatment took place.

POS (point-of-service) plan: A health plan allowing the member to choose to receive services from participating or non-participating providers. Some plans afford clients the choice to see the plan's HMO providers, PPO providers, or any licensed provider, and their coverage level will vary accordingly. If the client chooses an out-of network provider, coverage is at a lower level, and out-of-pocket expenses may be higher.

PPO (preferred provider organization): A managed care health plan with a network of providers which the health plan has contracted with to provide services at a discounted fee, in exchange for referrals. Clients can visit providers both in an out of the network, but pay a higher portion of the cost for an out-of-network provider. Members don't need to choose a primary care physician for coverage, and can visit specialists without a referral.

Pre-authorization: The process of obtaining approval from the health plan for sessions or hospital admission prior to start of treatment. .

Pre-certification: See Pre-authorization.

Pre-existing condition: A health condition (other than pregnancy) that was diagnosed or treated within six months prior to the client's enrollment in a new health plan (or a condition for which a reasonable person would have sought medical advice). Many insurance plans will not cover pre-existing conditions. Some will only cover them after a waiting period.

Preferred provider organization plan: See PPO

Premium: The amount the client or employer pays monthly in exchange for health insurance coverage.

Primary care physician (PCP): A client's main physician, usually a family or general practitioner, internist, or pediatrician, who provides a broad range of routine medical services and refers clients to specialists, hospitals, and other providers as needed. Some health plans require that the client has a PCP, and may require a PCP's referral to obtain services from other providers.

Prior authorization: See Pre-authorization.

Provider: A licensed health care facility, program, agency, physician, or other health professional that delivers health care services.

Provider network: A panel of providers contracted by a health plan to deliver medical services to the enrollees. The providers usually agree to accept a fee discount, and to file claims on behalf of the client.

Provider panel: See Provider network

Quality assurance: The steps taken by a managed care health plan to ensure quality of care, including provider credentialing and monitoring of provider care.

Recredentialing: A process used by a managed care company in which a network provider's information is updated and credentials are re-reviewed and matched against the credentials required to participate in the provider network. This is often done at regular intervals, such as annually.

Retro-authorization: An authorization for treatment given by an insurance company after the date of service.

SED (serious emotional disturbance): In certain state parity laws, children are afforded mental health coverage which is equal to that of medical coverage if they have diagnoses which meet the criteria in the state's parity law for "serious emotional disturbance."

Self-funded/self-insured plan: This is a type of health plan that is self-funded by the employer. Some plans contract with insurance carriers for claims processing and other administrative services, others may be self-administered. With self-funded plans, federal law (instead of state law) applies, and the benefits may be different from non-self-funded insurance plans.

Severe mental illness (SMI): This term is used in some state parity laws. In these state laws, only clients with a diagnosis that qualifies as a "severe mental illness" may be entitled to coverage that is equal to (at parity with) the coverage the plan offers for medical claims.

Single-case agreement: See Ad hoc.

SMI : See Severe mental illness.

Split-year claims: Claims that have charges from two or more years on the form.

Subscriber: The individual or dependent who is enrolled and eligible for coverage under a health plan.

Superbill: A list of charges and payments made for healthcare services provided. This may be given to a client to submit to their insurance plan for reimbursement. Also known as a statement or invoice.

Third-party administrator (TPA): An individual or firm hired by the employer to handle claims processing, pay providers, and manage other functions related to health insurance.

Third-party payer: Any payer for health care services other than the client. Examples include insurance companies and the federal government.

Transitional benefits/plans: When an employer changes insurance carriers, transition plans enable clients already in treatment to transition to a provider in the new network. They give the client and his current provider a specific number of days to contact the insurance company in order to discuss the client's treatment plan and to obtain authorization to continue treatment at the network benefit level for a specified period of time, or to transition to a professional in the new network.

TRICARE: The Defense Department's managed care plan for military dependents and retirees.

Usual, customary and reasonable (UCR) charges: The amount that the insurance company has determined is reasonable for a particular service, taking into account the usual fees for similar providers in your geographical area. The UCR is the maximum the plan will pay for any service.

Utilization: Measurement of the use of health insurance by employees of an insured employer, stated in terms of the average number of claims per employee.

Utilization management/review (UM/UR): The processes by which an insurance plan reviews a provider's treatment requests to determine whether care decisions are appropriate and to make reimbursement decisions, with a view to contain costs and monitor quality of care. This review may take place before, during, or after services have been rendered.

APPENDIX E
Sample Treatment Agreement

Barbara Griswold, LMFT
Licensed Marriage and Family Therapist (MFC27210)
4100 Moorpark Avenue #116, San Jose, California 95117
(408) 985-0846 (Emergencies 408-345-0552)

TREATMENT AGREEMENT

FEES: The fee per 50-minute session is $_____ (except for the first session, which is $_____). This is payable at the time of our session, unless I have agreed to bill your insurance plan.

CANCELLATIONS: You will be charged $_____ for missed sessions or those cancelled without 24-hour notice, except in cases of sudden illness or family emergency. Note: <u>Insurance plans will not pay for missed or late-cancelled sessions</u>. If I forget an appointment, I owe you a free session.

INSURANCE: If I am billing your insurance plan, you must pay your portion of the charges (the copayment) and any deductible at the time of the session. While I may submit insurance claims for you, you are still responsible for any portion of the fee not paid by your insurance plan.

<u>Please sign the following, if using your insurance plan or Employee Assistance Program</u>:
"I authorize the release of any information (Including treatment summaries and diagnosis) necessary to process insurance or Employee Assistance claims, or to request additional sessions.
I authorize payment of benefits to be made to Barbara Griswold, LMFT for services provided."
(Sign here)_____
(If applicable, second client sign here)_____

CONFIDENTIALITY: What you say in therapy, your records and your attendance are confidential, except:
- When you give written permission to release information
- When your records are subpoenaed for legal reasons
- When reporting is required or allowed by law (ex. suspected child abuse or neglect, extreme danger to self, suspected elder abuse, or danger to others)
- Other exceptions as outlined in my *Notice of Privacy Practices*

IN AN EMERGENCY: Leave a message on my answering machine, then call my 24-hour answering service, and state it is urgent that you reach me. The service will attempt to reach me, or another licensed therapist. In an emergency, go to your local emergency room or dial 911.

ENDINGS: You may end therapy at any time. A final phone call or session is requested for closure.

DISCLAIMERS: It is understood that any agreements made are between you and I only. The other therapists in the suite operate independent practices, and are not responsible for your care. I also cannot be responsible for the care provided by professionals or groups that I refer you to.

PRIVACY POLICY: By signing below, you acknowledge receipt of my *Notices of Privacy Practices*. This Notice provides information about how I may use and disclose your private health information. I encourage you to read it carefully. My Notice is subject to change; if changed, I will give you a revised Notice. If you have left treatment, you may obtain the revised notice from me at the above address.

If you have any questions about the Notice or any of the above, please feel free to ask.

_____	_____	_____
Signature	Printed Name	Date
_____	_____	_____
Signature, second client	Printed Name, second client	Date

Sample Invoice/Superbill

Barbara Griswold, LMFT

LICENSED MARRIAGE & FAMILY THERAPIST
4100 MOORPARK AVE. #116, SAN JOSE, CA 95117
TEL 408-985-0846   **EMAIL** BARBGRIS@AOL.COM

INVOICE DATE:_____/_____/_____

Client:	Birthdate: / /
Address:	
SSN or Plan ID:	Group # :

Insured/Responsible Party (if other):	Birthdate: / /
Address:	
Insured Plan ID or SSN:	Group # :

Date	Place of Service Code	CPT Code	Service Description or Payment Type	Diagnosis Code	Charges	Credits

Make Payment To:
☐ Client: _____
☐ Other: _____
☐ Barbara Griswold, LMFT

Previous Balance	$
New Charges	$
New Credits	$
Total Owed	$
Date Due	

Barbara C. Griswold, M.S., LMFT

Licensed Marriage & Family Therapist, MFC27210
TIN: XXXXXXXX   NPI: XXXXXXXX

APPENDIX G
Sample Service Record

Client Name: _Jack Klutz_   Diagnosis: _$309.81,305.20_   Co-pay: _$15_
Sessions Authorized: _8_ Start: _1/1/08_ Expires: _12/31/08_ Auth: _1005678_   Discount: _$33_
Sessions Authorized: ___ Start: _____ Expires: _____ Auth: _____   Deduct: _$0_
Sessions Authorized: ___ Start: _____ Expires: _____ Auth: _____   Ins Pays: _$52/ses._

Service Date	Ses #	Client Seen	Service Description	Fee Charged (may be Contract rate)	Credit	Ct. Copay	Ct. Owes Total	Ins. Owes For Ses.	Ins. Owes Total	Did Ins. Pay?
2/1/2008	1 of 8	Jack	Intake Ses.	$75.00	$15.00	$15.00	$0.00	$60.00	$60.00	√
2/8/2008	2 of 8	Jack	Individual Ses.	$67.00	$13.40	$13.40	$0.00	$53.60	$113.60	√
2/15/2008	3 of 8	Jack & Jill	Couples Ses.	$75.00	$0.00	$15.00	$15.00	$60.00	$173.60	√
2/22/2008	4 of 8	Jack	Individual Ses.	$67.00	$28.40	$13.40	$0.00	$53.60	$208.00	√
3/1/2008	—	—	Bill Ins for 2/08	—	—	—	$0.00	—	$227.20	—
3/15/2008	—	—	Ins. Pd. 2/08	—	$227.20	—	$0.00	—	$0.00	—

APPENDIX H
Sample Self-Pay Agreement

ও ৪

I, _____ (client name), have been notified by my

provider, _____ (provider name), or by my insurance

plan representative, _____ (representative's name), at my

health plan, _____ (insurance plan's name), that my

treatment starting on _____ (date) will not be paid for by my health plan

because it

    ____ is not a covered benefit under my benefit plan

    ____ is no longer covered by my benefit plan because my health plan has
        determined that the treatment does not meet the plan's standards for
        medical necessity

    ____ is no longer covered, as my benefits to see this provider for this service have
        been exhausted or terminated

If this is the result of a decision by my health plan, I have been informed about the reason, am aware of my plan's formal clinical appeal process, and have elected not to appeal, or am in the process of appealing this decision. Instead, and/or in the meantime, I have chosen to continue treatment with my provider on a self-pay basis starting _____ (date), which is no earlier than the date I have signed this form. I agree to pay the full amount of $_____ (amount) for _____ (services) on an out-of-pocket basis, and I understand I will not be reimbursed by my insurance unless I am successful on appeal.

I agree that the provider may bill and collect charges for the proposed services at his/her full fee-for-service rate. The plan maximum that applies to medically necessary covered services will not apply and will not limit the amount I may become obligated to pay for the proposed services.

This self-pay agreement applies only to the service listed above. If I move to another level of care, authorization may need to be obtained or another self-pay agreement signed.

I have read and understand this agreement. By signing this agreement, I know that I am creating a binding contract that is legally enforceable against me by the provider.

_____   _____
Signature of participant   Date

_____   _____
Signature of witness   Date

Index

ஐ எ

154

Book Order Form

ಇ ಅ

Two easy ways to order!

1) **Online:** Order at www.NavigatingtheInsuranceMaze.com

2) **By mail:** Mail this page with check or money order
made payable to Paper Street Press to

Paper Street Press
533 Patton Avenue, San Jose, CA 95128-2151
Telephone: (408) 985-0846

Please send me _____ copies of *Navigating the Insurance Maze:*
The Therapist's Complete Guide to Working with Insurance –
And Whether You Should.

_____ Book(s) at $29.95 each = $_____._____
  (#)   (we'll pay sales tax)
Shipping (see below) = $_____._____

TOTAL: $_____._____

U.S. Shipping: Please add $4.00 for the first book and
$2.00 for each additional book to cover shipping.

Orders are usually filled within 48 hours. Fees may be imposed on returned checks.

Please contact me regarding:
- ☐ Public speaking/training seminars
- ☐ Individual or small group consultations
- ☐ Put me on the mailing list for your free insurance e-mail newsletter

Name: _____

Mailing Address:_____

City:_____ State:_____ Zip:_____

Telephone: (____)_____ Alternate Phone: (____)_____

E-mail address:_____

157